Viktor Frankl's Contribution to Spirituality and Aging

Viktor Frankl's Contribution to Spirituality and Aging has been co-published simultaneously as *Journal of Religious Gerontology*, Volume 11, Numbers 3/4 2000.

The *Journal of Religious Gerontology* Monographic "Separates" (formerly *Journal of Religion & Aging*)*

Below is a list of "separates," which in serials librarianship means a special issue simultaneously published as a special journal issue or double-issue *and* as a "separate" hardbound monograph. (This is a format which we also call a "DocuSerial.")

"Separates" are published because specialized libraries or professionals may wish to purchase a specific thematic issue by itself in a format which can be separately cataloged and shelved, as opposed to purchasing the journal on an on-going basis. Faculty members may also more easily consider a "separate" for classroom adoption.

"Separates" are carefully classified separately with the major book jobbers so that the journal tie-in can be noted on new book order slips to avoid duplicate purchasing.

Routledge
Taylor and Francis Group
270 Madison Avenue
New York, NY 10016

Routledge
Taylor and Francis Group
2 Park Square
Milton Park, Abingdon
Oxon OX14 4RN

Viktor Frankl's Contribution to Spirituality and Aging, edited by Melvin A. Kimble, PhD (Vol. 11, No. 3/4, 2000) *Presents varying professional perspectives on the application of Frankl's logotherapy for ministry with older adults. Addresses issues such as death and dying, dementia and depression, and the spiritual meaning of aging.*

Aging in Chinese Society: A Holistic Approach to the Experience of Aging in Taiwan and Singapore, edited by Homer Jernigan and Margaret Jernigan (Vol. 8, No. 3, 1992) *"A vivid introduction to aging in these societies. . . Case studies illustrate the interaction of religion, personality, immigration, modernization, and aging." (Clinical Gerontologist)*

Spiritual Maturity in the Later Years, edited by James J. Seeber (Vol. 7, No. 1/2, 1991) *"An excellent introduction to the burgeoning field of gerontology and religion." (Southwestern Journal of Theology)*

Gerontology in Theological Education: Local Program Development, edited by Barbara Payne and Earl D. C. Brewer* (Vol. 6, No. 3/4, 1989) *"Directly relevant to gerontological education in other contexts and to applications in the educational programs and other work of church congregations and community agencies for the aging." (The Newsletter of the Christian Sociological Society)*

Gerontology in Theological Education, edited by Barbara Payne and Earl D. C. Brewer* (Vol. 6, No. 1/2, 1989) *"An excellent resource for seminaries and anyone interested in the role of the church in the lives of older persons. . . . must for all libraries." (David Maldonado, DSW, Associate Professor of Church & Society, Southern Methodist University, Perkins School of Theology)*

Religion, Aging and Health: A Global Perspective, compiled by the World Health Organization, edited by William M. Clements* (Vol. 4, No. 3/4, 1989) *"Fills a long-standing gap in gerontological literature. This book presents an overview of the interrelationship of religion, aging, and health from the perspective of the world's major faith traditions that is not available elsewhere . . . " (Stephn Sapp, PhD, Associate Professor of Religious Studies, University of Miami, Coral Gables, Florida)*

New Directions in Religion and Aging, edited by David B. Oliver* (Vol. 3, No. 1/2, 1987) *"This book is a telescope enabling us to see the future. The data of the present provides a solid foundation for seeing the future." (Dr. Nathan Kollar, Professor of Religious Studies and Founding Chair, Department of Gerontology, St. John Fisher College; Adjunct Professor of Ministerial Theology, St. Bernard's Institute)*

The Role of the Church in Aging, Volume 3: Programs and Services for Seniors, edited by Michael C. Hendrickson* (Vol. 2, No. 4, 1987) *"Experts explore an array of successful programs for the elderly that have been implemented throughout the United States in order to meet the social, emotional, religious, and health needs of the elderly."*

The Role of the Church in Aging, Volume 2: Implications for Practice and Service, edited by Michael C. Hendrickson* (Vol. 2, No. 3, 1986) *"Filled with important insight and state-of-the-art concepts that reflect the cutting edge of thinking among religion and aging professionals."* (Rev. James W. Ellor, DMin, AM, CSW, ACSW, Associate Professor, Department Chair, Human Service Department, National College of Education, Lombard, Illinois)

The Role of the Church in Aging, Volume 1: Implications for Policy and Action, edited by Michael C. Hendrickson* (Vol. 2, No. 1/2, 1986) *"Reviews the current status of the religious sector's involvement in the field of aging and identifies a series of strategic responses for future policy and action."*

Published by

The Haworth Pastoral Press®, 10 Alice Street, Binghamton, NY 13904-1580

The Haworth Pastoral Press® is an imprint of The Haworth Press, Inc., 10 Alice Street, Binghamton, NY 13904-1580 USA.

Viktor Frankl's Contribution to Spirituality and Aging has been co-published simultaneously as *Journal of Religious Gerontology* ™, Volume 11, Numbers 3/4 2000.

The development, preparation, and publication of this work has been undertaken with great care. However, the publisher, employees, editors, and agents of The Haworth Press and all imprints of The Haworth Press, Inc., including The Haworth Medical Press® and Pharmaceutical Products Press®, are not responsible for any errors contained herein or for consequences that may ensue from use of materials or information contained in this work. Opinions expressed by the author(s) are not necessarily those of The Haworth Press, Inc.

Cover design by Thomas J. Mayshock Jr.

Library of Congress Cataloging-in-Publication Data

Viktor Frankl's contribution to spirituality and aging/Melvin A. Kimble, editor.
    p. cm.
    Includes bibliographical references and index.
    ISBN 0-7890-1155-7 (alk. paper)–ISBN 0-7890-1156-5 (alk. paper)
    1. Frankl, Viktor Emil–Contributions in pastoral counseling of the aged. 2. Frankl, Viktor Emil–Contributions in church work with the aged. 3. Frankl, Viktor Emil–Contributions in spirituality. 4. Aged–Pastoral counseling of 5. Church work with the aged. 6. Spirituality. I. Kimble, Melvin.

BV4435.V55 2001
259.3′092–dc21
                                                     00-067348

Viktor Frankl's Contribution to Spirituality and Aging

Melvin A. Kimble, PhD
Editor

Viktor Frankl's Contribution to Spirituality and Aging has been co-published simultaneously as *Journal of Religious Gerontology*, Volume 11, Numbers 3/4 2000.

Routledge
Taylor & Francis Group
www.routledgementalhealth.com

Indexing, Abstracting & Website/Internet Coverage

This section provides you with a list of major indexing & abstracting services. That is to say, each service began covering this periodical during the year noted in the right column. Most Websites which are listed below have indicated that they will either post, disseminate, compile, archive, cite or alert their own Website users with research-based content from this work. (This list is as current as the copyright date of this publication.)

Abstracting, Website/Indexing Coverage ...... Year When Coverage Began

- *Abstracts in Social Gerontology: Current Literature on Aging* 1991

- *Abstracts of Research in Pastoral Care & Counselling* 1991

- *AGEINFO CD-ROM* 1994

- *AGELINE Database* 1994

- *Applied Social Sciences Index & Abstracts (ASSIA)*
  (Online: ASSI via Data-Star) (CD-Rom: ASSIA Plus) 1994

- *Brown University Geriatric Research Application Digest*
  "Abstracts Section" 1994

- *BUBL Information Service, an Internet-based Information*
  Service for the Uk higher education community
  <URL: http://bubl.ac.uk/> 1999

- *Christian Periodical Index, The* 1992

- *CNPIEC Reference Guide: Chinese National Directory*
  of Foreign Periodicals 1995

(continued)

Special Bibliographic Notes related to special journal issues
(separates) and indexing/abstracting:

- indexing/abstracting services in this list will also cover material in any "separate" that is co-published simultaneously with Haworth's special thematic journal issue or DocuSerial. Indexing/abstracting usually covers material at the article/chapter level.
- monographic co-editions are intended for either non-subscribers or libraries which intend to purchase a second copy for their circulating collections.
- monographic co-editions are reported to all jobbers/wholesalers/approval plans. The source journal is listed as the "series" to assist the prevention of duplicate purchasing in the same manner utilized for books-in-series.
- to facilitate user/access services all indexing/abstracting services are encouraged to utilize the co-indexing entry note indicated at the bottom of the first page of each article/chapter/contribution.
- this is intended to assist a library user of any reference tool (whether print, electronic, online, or CD-ROM) to locate the monographic version if the library has purchased this version but not a subscription to the source journal.
- individual articles/chapters in any Haworth publication are also available through the Haworth Document Delivery Service (HDDS).

Viktor Frankl's Contribution
to Spirituality and Aging

CONTENTS

ABOUT THE EDITOR

Melvin A. Kimble, PhD, ThM, is Professor Emeritus of Pastoral Care and Director of the Center for Aging, Religion, and Spirituality (CARS) at Luther Seminary where he has been on the faculty for 35 years. Dr. Kimble is an ordained Lutheran pastor in the Evangelical Lutheran Church in America.

Dr. Kimble was a lifelong student of the late Dr. Viktor Frankl, receiving a scholarship to study with him at the University of Vienna and Poliklinik Hospital. He also worked with Frankl at the United States International University, San Diego, where he received his PhD.

In recognition for his pioneering contribution to the field of religious gerontology, the American Society on Aging (ASA) honored him with the Spirituality and Aging Award in March 2000. In April 1999, Dr. Kimble was the recipient of the Spirituality and Aging Award from the National Council on Aging (NCOA) and the National Interfaith Coalition on Aging (NICA). He also received the American College and Health Care Administrators Research Award in 1986 and the Educational Foundation of America Award in 1982.

About the Contributors

Paul J. Brat, MD, is a retired physician and former director of Health-Partners, St. Paul, Minnesota and Associate Director, Center for Aging, Religion and Spirituality.

Richard E. Close, MDiv, LICSW, practices psychotherapy at the Allina Medical Clinic in Cottage Grove, Minnesota. He is a degree candidate in the D.Min. program at Luther Seminary in St. Paul, Minnesota.

James W. Ellor, PhD, is Professor of Human Services and Coordinator of Gerontology Programs, National-Louis University, Wheaton, Illinois, and Associate Director, Center for Aging, Religion and Spirituality.

R. Darren Erisman is pastor at Peace Lutheran Church, Silvana, Washington.

Melvin A. Kimble, PhD, is Emeritus Professor of Pastoral Theology at Luther Seminary, St. Paul, Minnesota, and Director of the Center for Aging, Religion and Spirituality.

Susan H. McFadden, PhD, is Associate Professor of Psychology at the University of Wisconsin, Oshkosh and Associate Director, Center for Aging, Religion and Spirituality.

Scott C. Peterson is pastor at the Galata Lutheran Parish, Galata, Montana.

Robert Rost, DMin, is pastor of Nativity of Mary Catholic Church, Independence, Missouri, and Associate Director, Center for Aging, Religion and Spirituality.

James J. Seeber, PhD, is Professor of Sociology at Vandenberg University Air Force Base, and Cuesta College in San Luis Obispo, California, and Associate Director, Center for Aging, Religion and Spirituality.

A Personal Note by the Guest Editor

Melvin A. Kimble, PhD

Former Nazi concentration camp prisoner #119,104 died in Vienna, September 2, 1997. That former prisoner, a survivor of the infamous Auschwitz, was Dr. Viktor E. Frankl, who was born March 26, 1905. He lived longer than he ever thought he would–92 1/2 years–and remained creatively and intellectually productive to the very end of his life. His life epitomized his concept of "the defiant power of the human spirit."

His impact on the field of psychotherapy is still to be assessed. However, his impact on what Frankl labeled "the man on the street" is attested to by the global sales of his seminal book, *Man's Search for Meaning*, published in 1946 under its original English translation title, *From Death Camp to Existentialism*. This book, which introduced the concepts of logotherapy amidst the poignant saga of Dr. Frankl's account of concentration camp life, is now in its 73rd printing. It has been translated into some 25 languages including Japanese, Chinese, and Russian. It has sold nine million copies in the English edition and has been listed by the U.S. Library of Congress as one of the most influential books in America.

When Frankl died, I personally lost not only a mentor but a friend who had a primary role in profoundly shaping my professional and personal life, as well as that of my wife, JoAnne. I first "discovered" Viktor Frankl in 1959 in a graduate course in Contemporary Psychotherapy and Pastoral Counseling. When I completed my degree and moved on to accept a position as head chaplain at a mental hospital, I

Dr. Kimble is Director of Center for Aging, Religion and Spirituality (CARS), and Professor Emeritus of Pastoral Theology, Luther Seminary.

[Haworth co-indexing entry note]: "A Personal Note by the Guest Editor." Kimble, Melvin A. Co-published simultaneously in *Journal of Religious Gerontology* (The Haworth Pastoral Press, an imprint of The Haworth Press, Inc.) Vol. 11, No. 3/4, 2000, pp. 1-6; and: *Viktor Frankl's Contribution to Spirituality and Aging* (ed: Melvin A. Kimble) The Haworth Pastoral Press, an imprint of The Haworth Press, Inc., 2000, pp. 1-6. Single or multiple copies of this article are available for a fee from The Haworth Document Delivery Service [1-800-342-9678, 9:00 a.m. - 5:00 p.m. (EST). E-mail address: getinfo@haworthpressinc.com].

continued to be captured with his concepts and insights into the human condition and their relevance and helpfulness to the cross-section of patients to whom I ministered. It was at this point as a young clergy chaplain with a master's degree in counseling that I was youthfully bold and professionally naïve enough to write to Frankl and inquire concerning the possibility of my coming to study with him in Vienna. At that time (1959) he was Professor of Neurology and Psychiatry at the University of Vienna Medical School and Head of the Vienna Neurological Poliklinik Hospital. With no credentials or professional experience to commend me to his tutelage, I had no reason to expect the positive response that came from him by air-mail within ten days containing the gracious and astonishing message "Yes, I'd be honored to have you come and study with me."

Now my only problem was to find funds that would enable me to bring my wife, two young daughters and myself to Vienna for a year of study. But when a door of opportunity is open a crack and you proceed to push and walk through it all kinds of unexpected and exciting things sometimes happen. But that's another story! Suffice to state that for me it was the most life-changing and memorable year of my life.

Following his liberation from Auschwitz, Frankl returned to his beloved Vienna, where in 1946 he was appointed Head of the Vienna Neurological Poliklinik Hospital, a position he held for 25 years. He became Associate Professor of Neurology and Psychiatry at the University of Vienna Medical School and was appointed Full Professor in 1955. He has held various professorship and academic appointments in the United States including Harvard University, Southern Methodist University, Stanford University, and Duquesne University. In 1970 the United States International University, San Diego, established for him a chair of Logotherapy which is now known as "The Third Viennese School of Psychotherapy" (following Freud's psychoanalysis and Adler's individual psychology).

Frankl was the author of 33 books, many of which have been translated into some 25 languages. He was the recipient of 28 honorary doctorates from universities around the world. His native Austria conferred on him the highest honor of the Republic for scientific achievements and the Austrian Academy of Sciences made him an honorary member. He has been a guest lecturer at over 250 universities around the world including Argentina, Australia, Sri Lanka, India, Israel, Japan, Mexico, and South Africa.

Frankl made lecture presentations on three different visits to Luther Seminary, St. Paul, Minnesota where his audience included the members of the faculty and student body, as well as community health care professionals. On one such trip, as he was about to leave to return to Vienna, he wanted to pick up several items that at that time (1966) were not available in Vienna. We stopped at a Target Store whose spacious and overflowing shelves somewhat overwhelmed him. As we were going through the checkout line, he spotted paperback copies of *Man's Search for Meaning* on a nearby bookrack. I immediately thought he would be offended that the personal account of his suffering was being sold in the midst of deodorants, batteries, paints, and toothpaste. But he was delighted. He exclaimed, "This is exactly where I want my book to be displayed and sold–where the 'man in the street' can purchase it–not simply in some remote university book store." It was "the man on the street" that Frankl wanted to reach in his writing and often said that logotherapy was the wisdom of the common man.

The American Psychiatric Association bestowed upon him in 1985 the coveted Oskar Pfister award and the *American Journal of Psychiatry* described his work as "perhaps the most significant thinking since Freud and Adler."[1] The late eminent Harvard psychologist, Gordon Allport, labeled logotherapy "the most significant psychological movement of our day."[2] Grabiel Marcel said Frankl "expresses in an illuminating manner that which is properly understood as the existential question."[3]

Frankl's formulation of logotherapy had been set forth many years prior to his incarceration at Auschwitz even though publishers' blurbs on some of Frankl's books often imply that he formulated the tenets of logotherapy while he was a prisoner in the concentration camp. Frankl actually first used the term logotherapy in a public lecture in 1926 and the term first appeared in print in a publication in 1929. His experiences and suffering in the concentration camp served as a human laboratory as Frankl himself states, ". . . one big experiment–a crucial experiment . . . that proved to us that even under the most deprived, the most humiliating conditions, man can still remain man . . . It should prove to us what man is, and what he can become."[4]

Commenting on the success of logotherapy, Frankl said,

I do not deserve to be congratulated for whatever success logo-therapy has enjoyed. In a private audience granted to us by Pope Paul VI, I told him: 'While others may look at what I may have accomplished, or rather what turned out well by good fortune, I realize at such moments how much more I should have done, but failed to do. In other words, how much do I owe to God's grace, granted to me for all these years beyond the time I was forced to walk through the gates of Auschwitz.'[5]

In 1947 Frankl married Elenore (Elly) Katharina, nee Schwindt, a young nurse who worked at the Poliklinik. Their one child, Dr. Gabriele Vesely, has two children, Alexander and Katharina. They live in Vienna where they together continue the work of logotherapy at the Viktor Frankl Institute.

Victor Frankl did not reflect publicly on his own aging until his last book, *Viktor Frankl Recollections: An Autobiography*, where he wrote:

I don't mind getting old. As I say, aging doesn't bother me as long as I have reason to believe that I am maturing. Perhaps this is still going on, since now I see the flaws in a manuscript I finished two weeks ago.[6]

In the last analysis, getting old is an aspect of the transitoriness of human existence. But this transitoriness can be a strong motivation for our responsibleness–our recognition of responsibility as basic to human existence.[7]

The climax of my first year of study with Frankl was an invitation he extended to me (and my wife) to accompany him on a trip back to Auschwitz (Poland), that infamous concentration camp where he had suffered and lost so much. It was in that camp and those gas chambers where his young bride, and his brother and his parents died. Following his footsteps, as he made his torturous and painful trip through the camp, provided me with an indelible personal memory of Frankl. It was in this inhuman setting that Frankl later stated: " . . where everything unessential had been stripped from man, where everything which a person had–money, power, fame, luck–disappeared: while only that remained which man does not 'have' but which he must 'be.'

What remained was man himself who in the white heat of suffering and pain was melted down to the essentials, to the human in himself."[8] In that remarkable memorial speech which he delivered at the request of the Society of Physicians in Vienna, March 25, 1949, for the members who died in the years 1938-45, when the concept of "collective guilt" of all Germans was running rampant in so many nations, Frankl appealed for forgiveness rather than condemnation. He stated that all who engaged in a collective condemning of those who participated in or did nothing to stop that mass killing of Jews and others in concentration camps "must first prove that they themselves in such a situation would have been a hero."[9]

In this inspiring memorial address, Frankl poignantly and profoundly declared:

> What then is man? We ask again. He is a being who continuously decides what he is: a being who equally harbors the potential to descend to the level of an animal or to ascend to the life of a saint. Man is that being, who, after all, invented the gas chambers; but at the same time he is that being who entered into those same gas chambers with his head held high and with the 'Our Father' or the Jewish prayer of the dying on his lips.[10]

The author of this profound humane statement is the unique person we honor in this volume. His contributions to the field of psychotherapy and their implications for pastoral care and counseling have yet to be fully plumbed. His openness to multidisciplinary approaches to understanding the human condition has resulted in the tenets and concept of logotherapy being very adaptable and relevant to pastoral care with persons at every stage of life's journey.

Factors leading to this special volume are the continuing valuing of Frankl's logotherapy for ministry with older adults, particularly his vigorous affirmations of the spiritual dimension of humanity and the dignity and worth of every person, even when they face "the tragic triad of human existence: pain, guilt and death."

I hope that something of Frankl's genuine humanity as well as his scholarly theory are helpfully reflected in these pages.

NOTES

1. Viktor E. Frankl, *Man's Search for Ultimate Meaning* (New York: Insight Books, 1997), 188.

2. Viktor E. Frankl, *The Will to Meaning* (New York: New American Library/ The World Publishing Company, 1969), 180.

3. Ibid.

4. Viktor E. Frankl, *Psychotherapy and Existentialism* (New York: Washington Square Press, 1967), 110.

5. Viktor E. Frankl, *Viktor Frankl Recollections: An Autobiography* (New York: Insight Books, 1997), 124.

6. Ibid., 122-123.

7. Ibid., 124.

8. Frankl, *Psychotherapy and Existentialism*, 110.

9. Ibid., 111.

10. Ibid., 110.

Acknowledgments

The essays in this volume represent a variety of perspectives on the theory and clinical application of logotherapy, the School of Psychotherapy founded by Dr. Viktor E. Frankl. Six of the essays represent presentations made at a conference sponsored by the Center for Aging, Religion and Spirituality (CARS) held at Luther Seminary, St. Paul, Minnesota on July 17, 1999. The theme of the conference was "Viktor Frankl's Contribution to Gerontology" and focused on meaning issues confronting those engaging in ministry with older adults.

The contributors' summaries at the beginning of their essays present a succinct overview of their respective papers. Suffice to state that the collection of essays includes contributions from theorists as well as practitioners, from academicians as well as clinicians. Writers include a physician, a sociologist, a pastoral theologian, a psychologist, three parish pastors, two social workers, and two graduate students.

The reader may disagree with an interpretation of logotherapy by a contributor, but out of differing perspectives dialogue often emerges that enriches logotherapeutic theory. Frankl would have encouraged such dialogue because he wanted logotherapy to be an open system.

I want to express appreciation to the authors of these provocative essays and also to the CARS administrative staff who assisted in preparing and assembling this collection for publication, especially to Chad Christensen and Mee-Ock Park.

Melvin A. Kimble
CARS Center, St. Paul, MN
February, 2000

[Haworth co-indexing entry note]: "Acknowledgments." Kimble, Melvin A. Co-published simultaneously in *Journal of Religious Gerontology* (The Haworth Pastoral Press, an imprint of The Haworth Press, Inc.) Vol. 11, No. 3/4, 2000, p. 7; and: *Viktor Frankl's Contribution to Spirituality and Aging* (ed: Melvin A. Kimble) The Haworth Pastoral Press, an imprint of The Haworth Press, Inc., 2000, p. 7. Single or multiple copies of this article are available for a fee from The Haworth Document Delivery Service [1-800-342-9678, 9:00 a.m. - 5:00 p.m. (EST). E-mail address: getinfo@haworthpressinc.com].

Logotherapy: An Overview

Melvin A. Kimble, PhD
James W. Ellor, PhD

BASICS OF LOGOTHERAPY

Viktor Frankl is the founder of Logotherapy which has come to be called the Third Viennese School of Psychotherapy (after Freud's psychoanalysis and Adler's individual psychology). Logotherapy finds its philosophical roots in existentialism and phenomenology, its psychological roots in psychoanalysis and individual psychology, and its spiritual roots in a profound commitment to the human being as an irreducibly spiritual creature. It is perhaps in the area of the conception of the human being that Frankl's differences with those schools of thought which constitute the roots of Logotherapy can best be distinguished. The anthropology of a therapeutic system profoundly influences the entire system. Most psychology has grown from a view of humanity as a creature of biology fully explicable in terms of the commonalities between humanity and the rest of the living creatures.

Rev. Melvin A. Kimble is Professor Emeritus at Luther Seminary. Rev. James W. Ellor is Professor, National-Louis University.

This article was originally printed as a hand-out for a lecture presented by Viktor Frankl on the topic of aging, held at the Annual Meeting of the American Society on Aging, 1989, in Washington, DC. This event was sponsored by the Forum on Religion, Spirituality and Aging, The National Interfaith Coalition on Aging, Retirement Research Foundation, The American Association of Retired Persons, The Board of Social Ministry of the Evangelical Lutheran Church in America, and National-Louis University.

[Haworth co-indexing entry note]: "Logotherapy: An Overview." Kimble, Melvin A. and James W. Ellor. Co-published simultaneously in *Journal of Religious Gerontology* (The Haworth Pastoral Press, an imprint of The Haworth Press, Inc.) Vol. 11, No. 3/4, 2000, pp. 9-24; and: *Viktor Frankl's Contribution to Spirituality and Aging* (ed: Melvin A. Kimble) The Haworth Pastoral Press, an impirnt of The Haworth Press, Inc., 2000, pp. 9-24. Single or multiple copies of this article are available for a fee from The Haworth Document Delivery Service [1-800-342-9678, 9:00 a.m. - 5:00 p.m. (EST). E-mail address: getinfo@haworthpressinc.com].

Such a view tends to reduce concepts such as responsibility and meaning to complex expressions of biological urges or drives.

Frankl, convinced of the importance of an explicit conception of the nature of humanity, presents a well-developed anthropology in his writings. He speaks frequently of the nature of human beings. For Frankl, human beings are wonderfully complex, not to be reduced to a collection of drives and urges, not to be understood completely in terms of biology. Human beings are spiritual beings. By this, Frankl means that they are transcendent, not only over the world, but more importantly over self. *"Self-transcendence*, I would say, is the essence of existence; and existence, in turn, means the specifically human mode of being."[1] This essentially human way of being in the world has its core in the unconscious. Frankl finds that humans have both an instinctual unconscious and a spiritual unconscious. The latter gives rise to conscience which gives evidence of its unconscious source in its ability to relate to what is not yet, whereas the conscious mind can only relate to what is or what has been.

Frankl also states that human beings are unique. Each person is at the focus of an absolutely unique confluence of physical and spiritual currents which define the individual as completely and absolutely distinct from all other human beings. Thus one must learn to live as a responsible being expressing and responding to the distinctive self that is unlike all other selves. One must learn to bear the "otherness" of the human condition.

Frankl states that human beings are by nature responsible. The unique confluence of events which result in the distinct individuality of persons calls for a response, which can and should be answered affirmatively, responsibly. There is a call from outside, a call which expresses the meaning of individual lives and circumstances. The call requires an answer, a commitment to meaning, to purposeful rather than chaotic activity. The meaning is circumstantial, thus individual and unique in each person's situation. "Being human is being conscious and being responsible, culminating in a synthesis of both–namely in one's consciousness of his responsibleness."[2]

Despite the absolute and unique individuality of persons, human beings are essentially relational. "Being human means relating, and being directed, to something other than oneself."[3] This other is the logos, or meaning. In this sense, meaning is both a part of the person, but at the same time larger than any one person, as meaning can be shared between persons. Real encounter, for Frankl, is triadic and involves the logos as well as the two persons involved. Without some shared meaning, the apparent encounter and ensuing dialogue between two persons is really only "a mutual monologue" or "mutual self-expression."

Human beings are limited. This is a two-fold limitation. First, is the limit of one's destiny, which sums up the unique set of opportunities and influences which converge upon the individual at any particular time. One cannot actualize opportunities which are not present, nor can one respond and be responsible for other than the call of the logos as expressed within the particular set of circumstances.[4] Secondly each human being is limited by death which sooner or later will put an end to opportunities and responsibilities. Far from seeing death as that which renders all of the acts of life ultimately meaningless, and thus as the cause for despair, Frankl sees death as that which gives direction to life, charging each moment with potential which would not be possible if there is an infinite succession of moments to come. Today is the day, the appointed hour. Such thought would be meaningless were it not for death and the closure it brings. The absolute boundary to our possibilities charges the present with responsibility and meaning. "The meaning of human existence is based upon its irreversible quality."[5] And "death itself is what makes life meaningful."[6]

Human beings are free, but not in the sense of absolute freedom. Such freedom is mythical, actually being chaos. Rather humans may use their transcendence to observe that situation which includes all that impinges upon them at a particular moment, and having observed, they may take a stand for or a stand against the world. Indeed a human being may even take a stand against himself/herself. Freedom is not in the circumstances. It is not something which is possessed and which might be lost. Freedom is the essence of what human beings are by virtue of being human.[7]

An implication of the freedom of humanity is the fact that human beings are more than the sum of heredity and environment. Human beings are the product of both their genetic and situational history as well as the decisions that they have made. Human beings are committing beings, responding to their destiny with affirmation or denial. A human being is "that entity which has freed itself from whatever has determined it (determined it as biological-sociological type); that entity, in other words, that transcends all these determinants either by conquering them and shaping them, or by deliberately submitting to them."[8]

Frankl's anthropology, in summary, is absolutely opposed to reductionist anthropologies which perceive humans as driven by instincts or controlled by the will to power. Rather he sees humans as free to transcend that which might determine them through the transcendence of the logos and the freedom to adopt an attitude which brings the determinants within the scope of meaning.

Logotherapy is to be contrasted with other therapies with respect to the goals of therapy. Frankl states that the alleged goal of psychoanalysis is to bring about an acceptable compromise between the demands of the unconscious and the requirements of reality. The goal is to adjust the individual to the surrounding circumstances. Individual psychology is more ambitious and hopeful. "Beyond mere adjustment, it demands of the patient a courageous reshaping of reality . . ."[9] Logotherapy has as its goal the fulfillment of the individual, a breakthrough into another dimension which allows the individual to transcend the boundaries and constraints of life which prove unchangeable. Thus even the most severe situations of life may prove rich in meaning and fulfillment.

The relationship between anthropology and therapeutic goals is quite clear. Psychoanalysis, operating with an anthropology which sees human beings as organic mechanisms, seeks to adjust the mechanism to fit within the larger mechanisms of society and the cosmos. Individual psychology, with its appreciation of human courage and capacity for growth, seeks adjustment of the larger systems to allow and encourage growth and development of individuals. Logotherapy, with an even higher view of humanity focused upon transcendence and responsibility, seeks human accomplishment even when both inner and outer adjustments leave a gap between the opportunities allowed by destiny and the desires of the individual. Logotherapy seeks to make persons aware of their freedom of response to all aspects of their destiny. The person is shown the possibility of conscious and responsible activity in his/her life situation. The goal is to have the person recognize that there are options in the most oppressive situations, and that one is responsible for one's action/inaction even if the only possible action is the adoption of an attitude. Logotherapy does not say to what or for what a person is responsible. To lead a person beyond the point where "he profoundly understands his existence as responsibility, is neither possible nor necessary."[10] When Logotherapy brings a person to the point of discerning for herself/himself the meaning of her/his destiny, a creative and concrete response will occur. The basic human orientation toward meaningful existence asserts itself when the obstacles have been cleared away.

The goal of Logotherapy in other words is to stimulate the will to meaning. Frankl finds that human beings are oriented toward meaning and seek meaning in all their circumstances. Both the will to pleasure and the will to power derive from the will to meaning.[11] Above the plane of human existence there is a level of supra-meaning which speaks to the human conscience concerning the meaning of each person's life. Belief in such a supra-meaning is "of the foremost psychotherapeutic and psychohygienic importance."[12] A person who believes in such an ultimate meaning lives a life open to the call of such meaning upon conscience, and is prepared to commit herself/himself to a meaningful response to destiny. At the human level, meaning is always individual and unique. Because meaning is contextual, it varies from individual to individual and from day to day. Being limited and finite, the individual can never perceive the ultimate meaning which gathers up the unique individual meanings into a unique whole.

Meaning is not identical with nor dependent upon success. Personal fulfillment is independent of success. Work and other activity gain meaning just so far as they are the expression of those personal and specific elements which combine to define the unique individual. Meaningful activity expresses or embodies the unique confluence of events, influences and decisions which make up the human.

Meaning is objective in that it comes from outside and may confront the self, standing ahead of and setting the pace for the self. Thus meaning may confront, as well as affirm. Meaning, as the projection from another dimension, ultimately exceeds the scope of rational exploration. Frankl refers to Pascal's remark that the branch can never grasp the meaning of the whole tree.[13]

Frankl believes that when the obstacles have been removed, each person will find that the meaning of his/her situation is readily apparent, and that the person will then automatically react with a creative and concrete response. Frankl supposes that it is neither necessary nor possible to go beyond awakening the individual to her/his existence as a responsible being. The contextual nature of meaning implies that one cannot point out the specific meaning for another. Each must see the meaning of his/her own context. The role of the Logotherapist, Frankl suggests, like an opthamologist, does not tell us what to see but simply corrects our ability to see.

APPLICATIONS OF LOGOTHERAPY TO AGING AND OLDER ADULTHOOD

Logotherapy accepts a priori that striving to find meaning in life is a primary motivational force throughout the life cycle. The vitality of a person's life at every stage depends upon his or her supply of meanings. There is increasing evidence to suggest that the crisis of aging appears to be a crisis of meaning. The challenge of older adulthood is to make sense of life at a stage when changes and losses occur with bewildering and sometimes overwhelming frequency and intensity. Older persons require a sense of meaning in their lives in order to cope successfully with the eroding and debilitating diminishments that aging and growing old often introduce.

Many persons who have worked in long term care have encountered the individual who questions why they continue to live. Mrs. Smith is 96 years old. She has multiple chronic impairments including arthritis and a right brain stroke. She is functionally bed bound. Whenever anyone stops to talk to her, she frequently asks the question, "Why won't God let me die?" Her explanation of this statement reflects her pain. "I am 96 years old. My husband is dead, my parents are dead, my 6 brothers and sisters are all dead, my three children are all dead, even two of my twelve grandchildren are dead. All of my friends are dead and even the nurse who used to take care of me has taken a job somewhere else and is no longer here. I am of no earthly use to anyone . . . Why won't God let me die?" To respond to Mrs. Smith by arguing theology and trying to rationalize God's purpose for everyone, or to argue any position that tries to rationalize God's actions, is to completely miss the point. The Mrs. Smiths in our nursing homes and community are struggling with the crisis of meaning.

It has been observed that the enormous gains in longevities as a result of medical and technological progress have been accompanied ". . . by widespread spiritual malaise . . . and confusion over the meaning and purpose of life–particularly in old age . . . "[14] Such findings seem to confirm Frankl's observation that: "The truth is that as the struggle for survival has subsided, the question has emerged:

survival for what? Even more people today have the means to live but no meaning to live for." [15]

There is an imperative need for a wider frame of reference in the study of aging that allows for the full exploration of the question of meaning in old age. The natural science model has in many respects served gerontology well, but not well enough. It is powerless to reveal to us the meaning of our lives. What is required is a paradigm that utilizes a phenomenological approach to aging and its processes and moves beyond an empirical research model which is limited to a positivistic focus in biomedical and social conditions of aging. The framework of Viktor Frankl's Logotherapy provides a phenomenological approach for making the formulation of meaning a legitimate pursuit of inquiry.

Sources of Personal Meaning

Personal meanings do not develop in a vacuum. A phenomenological analysis of the immediate data of the actual life experience of an individual reveals sources of meaning in that person's life. Frankl maintains that life can be made meaningful in a threefold way:

> First, through *what we give* (in terms of creative works); second by *what we take* from the world (in terms of our experiencing values); and third, through the *stand we take* toward a fate we no longer can change (an incurable disease, an inoperable cancer, or the like). [16]

Meaning is not invented but discovered. One can give meaning to our lives by realizing *creative values*, that is, by achieving tasks. One can also give meaning to our lives by realizing *experiential* values, "by experiencing the Good, the True, and the Beautiful, or by knowing one single human being in all of his uniqueness. And to experience one human being as unique means to love him." [17] Even when those experiences are impossible, "a man can still give his life a meaning by the way he faces his fate, his distress." [18] A person realizes values by attitudes toward destined or inescapable suffering. These *attitudinal* values, as Frankl calls them, give a person, when being confronted with a hopeless situation, a last opportunity to fulfill a meaning–"to realize the highest value to fulfill even the deepest meaning–and that is the meaning of suffering." [19]

New Fields of Meaning

Older persons may need to learn how to redefine their values and goals and understand how the sources of meaning in their lives have shifted. A person's life is never without meaning. It is a matter of refocusing and coming to a new understanding of the sources and shapes of those meanings. Logotherapy provides reorientation which helps older persons to view old age, not as a stage of stagnation and absence of meaning, but of new growth and development characterized more by "being" rather than "doing." This "increased interiority of the personality," as Bernice Neugarten described it,[20] may be a proverbial gold mine of new meanings waiting to be discovered at this stage of life.

Furthermore, it is a tenet of Logotherapy that life's transitoriness does not in the least detract from its meaningfulness. Life holds meaning, in whatever circumstance, until the last breath. Frankl reflecting on his role as a medical doctor writes:

> Day by day I am confronted with people who are incurable, men who become senile, and women who remain sterile. I am besieged by their cry for an answer to the question of an ultimate meaning to suffering . . . But if there is meaning, it is unconditional meaning, and neither suffering nor dying can detract from it. And what our patients need is unconditional faith in unconditional meaning.[21]

The Meaning of Time

A marked characteristic of Logotherapy is that it takes time seriously. Memory emphasizes time lapsed. In remembering, persons take responsibility for values actualized and values denied. The individual is understood as one responsible for his or her life story and the telling of it.[22] Logotherapy's understanding of time is poignantly set forth by Frankl:

> All that is good and beautiful in the past is safely preserved in that past. On the other hand, so long as life remains, all guilt and all evil are still "redeemable" . . . this is not the case of a finished film . . . or an already existent film which is merely being unrolled. Rather, the film of this world is just being "shot." Which

means nothing more or less than that the future–happily–still remains to be shaped; that is, it is at the disposal of man's responsibility.[23]

Once a possibility has been made into a reality, it is delivered safely into "the granary of the past." "The past is precisely that which cannot be taken away."[24]

The Tragic Triad

For Frankl, the tragic triad of pain, guilt, and death are inevitable and inherent in human existence.[25] But, according to Logotherapy, it is the very transitoriness of human existence which constitutes an individual's responsibleness–the essence of existence. It is this two-fold understanding of finiteness in terms of fallibility and mortality which add to life's worthwhileness " . . . since only in the face of guilt does it make sense to improve, and only in the face of death is it meaningful to act."[26]

Defiant Power of the Human Spirit

One of Logotherapy's most helpful contributions to gerontology is its stress on the "defiant power of the human spirit."[27] While recognizing the holistic nature of the human being, the Logotherapist appeals to what lies beyond the person's psycho-physical nature–the spirit. The spiritual core of a person is recognized as capable of taking a stand not only toward negative and painful external circumstances but also toward its own psychological character structure. Such recognition conveys to older persons a renewed awareness of self-worth and human dignity. Conversely, if they regard themselves as inadequate psychic mechanisms, with no control and responsibility for themselves, they have no capacity to transcend themselves or fashion meaning from their suffering.[28]

THE THERAPEUTIC USE OF MEANING WITH THE ELDERLY

Movement from the theoretical foundation of Logotherapy to the application of this approach to older adults will require the therapist to first get to know the person and his or her lived world. Like most therapeutic approaches, the Logotherapist needs to establish the empathic bond by listening to the client. In Logotherapy, however, the types of questions may vary from other approaches. Three areas of inquiry are important for the discovery of meaning. The first reflects the values of the individual. For the person who values kindness, meaning can be derived by being kind or receiving kindness. If the individual does not value hard work, or looks down on persons who do find meaning in working hard, then clearly the individual is not going to find meaning in this type of activity. Missinne observes:[29]

> The older person, who either chooses not to or is not allowed to work, may be required to set aside the realization of creative values. Still, he or she has the opportunity to find deep meaning in the experiencing of beauty or loving relationships. If due to isolation and ill health, neither of these is possible, there is still what Frankl considers the highest achievement and, consequently, the deepest meaning available to an older person–the freedom of choosing one's response to this last challenge. How a person faces his own sufferings could be the highest value which will give meaning to his life.

For Frankl, values are transmitted by traditions. He sees these traditions as decaying in modern society. Frankl asserts: "Only values–which might be defined as universal meanings–can be affected by the decay of traditions."[30] While Frankl does not discredit the importance of values, he seems to find them lacking in many individuals. Frankl contends:

> One may say that instincts are transmitted through the genes, and values are transmitted through traditions, but that meanings, being unique, are a matter of personal discovery. They must be sought and found by oneself, and such discovery of unique meanings, as we now understand, will be possible even if all universal values disappear totally. To put it succinctly: the values are dead–long live the meanings.[31]

Thus, Frankl feels that meaning can be discovered by the individual, even if that person cannot identify his or her values.

As the therapist becomes more acquainted with the older adult, he or she will keep track of both the values discussed by the client as well as the choices that the individual has made. The choices made by the individual reflect a second area where Logotherapy is somewhat different from many other approaches. Frankl writes:

> As a human phenomenon, however, freedom is all too human. Human freedom is finite freedom. Man is not free from conditions. But he is free to take a stand in regard to them. The conditions do not completely condition him. Within limits it is up to him whether or not he succumbs and surrenders to the conditions. He may as well rise above them and by so doing open up and enter the human dimension . . . Ultimately, man is not subject to the conditions that confront him; rather, these conditions are subject to his decision. Wittingly or unwittingly, he decides whether he will face up or give in, whether or not he will let himself be determined by the conditions.[32]

As the therapist listens to the client discuss his or her life, it can become clear that decisions have been made in response to the events and conditions of living over which the individual has indeed made choices. Helping the client to understand these choices may help the individual to see where he or she can now have choices that can render the individual greater control over a more meaningful future.

The third area of inquiry relates to the fact that while Frankl acknowledges that there is an ultimate meaning, there is also meaning within each event. As Missinne states: "The comprehension of infinite meaning in one's life is preceded by provisional or short term experiences which also give meaning to life."[33] While one can summarize the collection of the meanings of these single events into a larger generalization of meaning, it must be remembered that the smaller events have meaning as well. Indeed, because each experience for Frankl is a unique experience, it may be difficult to find the conceptual continuity that pulls together an ultimate meaning. As Reker and Wong point out:

> The zest and vitality of goal directed activities, the sweat of hard work and the joy of success, the excitement and satisfaction of engaging in intimate relationships, and the many personal experiences that give color, texture, and richness to the tapestry of life are the raw materials for present meaning. We create meaning

through choices and actions as we move through life, but we also discover meaning from many 'happenings' that come our way each day.[34]

As Frankl asserts: "This ultimate meaning necessarily exceeds and surpasses the finite intellectual capacities of man."[35]

As the therapeutic relationship moves from assessment to treatment, the therapist may need to help the client to discover meaning. As suggested earlier, Frankl explains that this can be done in three ways:

(1) by creating a work or doing a deed; (2) by experiencing something or encountering someone; and (3) by the attitude we take toward unavoidable suffering.[36]

In many ways, Logotherapy offers a different way to look at the difficulties or events of suffering that happen in life. Frankl suggests that

the emphasis on responsibleness is reflected in the categorical imperative of Logotherapy, which is: 'Live as if you were living already for the second time and as if you had acted the first time as wrongly as you are about to act now!'[37]

In this change of perception the individual moves from seeing their fate as unalterable to seeking the meaning in their suffering. It is important to note that Frankl does not suggest that "suffering is necessary to find meaning. I only insist that meaning is possible even in spite of suffering–provided, certainly, that the suffering is unavoidable."[38]

The actual techniques involved with older clients may include Socratic Dialogue, Dereflection, Paradoxical Intention, or the use of humor. Each of these approaches involves helping older adults to see a new way of examining the "difficulties" or hurts within their lives in order to discover the meaning that these events or feelings can have. It is important for the older adult to be able to see the possibility of finding meaning even if everyone that the client has ever known or cared about has died; to see the possibility of meaning even if they are suffering from incurable diseases. As Frankl maintains:

to see 'that unconditional meaning, however, is paralleled by the unconditional value of each and every person. It is that which warrants the indelible quality of the dignity of man. Just as life remains potentially meaningful under any conditions, even those which are most miserable, so too does the value of each and every person stay with him or her, and it does so because it is based on values that he or she has realized in the past, and is not contingent on the usefulness that he or she may or may not retain in the present.'[39]

CONCLUSION

Gerontologists will find in Logotherapy an ally for assisting them in confronting the humanity of their clients at the deepest level–the level of meaning. The Logotherapeutic tenet that self-transcendence is the essence of human existence opens the door to a deeper understanding of the human capacity to dedicate and commit oneself to something or someone beyond one's self. With its concept of dimensional ontology Logotherapy provides creative interpretations of the ontological differences and anthropological unity of personhood.[40] It enriches the understanding of meanings and values, of freedom and responsibility, of conscience and commitment, of decision and responsibleness, of suffering and faith. It exegetes what Rheinhold Niebuhr characterized as the basic question of life, namely, "the problem of meaning."[41] It dynamically focuses on what Paul Tillich pointed to when he wrote: "Man is ultimately concerned about his being and his meaning."[42]

In its recognition of the holistic nature of the human person, Logotherapy appeals to what lies beyond the psycho-physical nature of an older person. By emphasizing that a human being is not simply a psychosomatic organism, Logotherapy introduces an understanding of personhood which affirms one's capacity to find meaning in life in every stage of life, indeed, even in the midst of suffering and dying. Logotherapy attempts to construct a dynamic synthesis of the various dimensions of personhood and thereby communicates both realism and hope. It provides an understanding of life at all of its diverse stages, including old age, as life lived *sub specie aeternitatis.*

REFERENCES

1. Viktor E. Frankl, *Psychotherapy and Existentialism: Selected Papers on Logotherapy* (New York: Washington Square Press, 1967). 74.

2. Viktor E. Frankl, *The Unconscious God* (New York: Washington Square Press, 1975). 60.

3. Viktor E. Frankl, *The Unheard Cry for Meaning: Psychotherapy and Humanism* (New York: Washington Square Press, 1984). 66.

4. Viktor E. Frankl, *The Doctor and the Soul: From Psychotherapy to Logotherapy*, Revised and Expanded ed. (New York: Vintage Books, 1986). 75.

5. Ibid. 64.

6. Ibid. 74.

7. Ibid. 97.

8. Ibid. 86.

9. Ibid. 9.

10. Ibid. 275.

11. Viktor E. Frankl, *Psychotherapy and Existentialism: Selected Papers on Logotherapy* (New York: Washington Square Press, 1967). 6.

12. Viktor E. Frankl, *The Doctor and the Soul: From Psychotherapy to Logotherapy*, Revised and Expanded ed. (New York: Vintage Books, 1986). 33.

13. Viktor E. Frankl, *The Will to Meaning: Foundations and Applications of Logotherapy* (New York: A Meridian Book, 1988). 31.

14. Thomas R. Cole, "Aging, Meaning, and Well-Being: Musings of a Cultural Historian," *International Journal of Aging and Human Development* 19 (1984) 329.

15. Viktor E. Frankl, *The Unheard Cry for Meaning: Psychotherapy and Humanism* (New York: Washington Square Press, 1984). 21.

16. Viktor E. Frankl, *The Doctor and the Soul: From Psychotherapy to Logotherapy*, Revised and Expanded ed. (New York: Vintage Books, 1986). xii.

17. Viktor E. Frankl, *Psychotherapy and Existentialism: Selected Papers on Logotherapy* (New York: Washington Square Press, 1967). 14-15.

18. Viktor E. Frankl, *The Unheard Cry for Meaning: Psychotherapy and Humanism* (New York: Washington Square Press, 1984). 119-120.

19. Ibid. 35.

20. Bernice Neugarten et al., *Personality in Middle and Later Life* (New York: Atherton Press, 1964).

21. Viktor E. Frankl, *The Unheard Cry for Meaning: Psychotherapy and Humanism* (New York: Washington Square Press, 1984). 104-105.

22. Melvin A. Kimble, "Aging and the Search for Meaning," *Journal of Religion & Aging* Summer/Fall Vol. 6, no. 1/2 (1989). 31-32.

23. Viktor E. Frankl, *The Doctor and the Soul: From Psychotherapy to Logotherapy*, Revised and Expanded ed. (New York: Vintage Books, 1986). 34.

24. Viktor E. Frankl, *The Unheard Cry for Meaning: Psychotherapy and Humanism* (New York: Washington Square Press, 1984). 112.

25. Viktor E. Frankl, *The Doctor and the Soul: From Psychotherapy to Logotherapy*, Revised and Expanded ed. (New York: Vintage Books, 1986). 59.

26. Ibid.

27. Viktor E. Frankl, *Psychotherapy and Existentialism: Selected Papers on Logotherapy* (New York: Washington Square Press, 1967). 99.

28. Melvin A. Kimble, "Aging and the Search for Meaning," *Journal of Religion & Aging* Summer/Fall Vol. 6, no. 1/2 (1989). 33.

29. Leo E. Missinne and Judy Willeke-Kay, "Reflections on the Meaning of Life in Older Age," *Journal of Religion & Aging* Summer Vol 1., no. 4 (1985): 46.

30. Viktor E. Frankl, *The Unheard Cry for Meaning: Psychotherapy and Humanism* (New York: Washington Square Press, 1984). 41.

31. Ibid.

32. Ibid. 51. 52.

33. Leo E. Missinne and Judy Willeke-Kay, "Reflections on the Meaning of Life in Older Age," *Journal of Religion & Aging* Summer Vol 1., no. 4 (1985): 47.

34. Gary T. Reker and Paul T. P. Wong, "Aging as an Individual Process: Toward a Theory of Personal Meaning," found in *The Emergent Theories of Aging*, Ed. by James E. Birren and Vern L. Bengston (New York: Springer Publishing Co. 1988). 230.

35. Viktor E. Frankl, *Man's Search for Meaning* (New York: Washington Square Press, 1984). 141.

36. Ibid. 133.

37. Ibid. 131-132.

38. Ibid. 136.

39. Ibid. 176.

40. Ibid. 136-142.

41. Reinhold Niebuhr, *The Nature and Destiny of Man*, Vol. I (New York: Charles Scribner, 1953).

42. Paul Tillich, *The Courage to Be* (New Haven: Yale University Press, 1952).

REFERENCES TO LOOK FOR BY VIKTOR E. FRANKL

Viktor E. Frankl, *Psychotherapy and Existentialism: Selected Papers on Logotherapy* (New York: Washington Square Press, 1967).

Viktor E. Frankl, "Determinism and Humanism," *Humanities* 7, no. 1 (1971): 23-36.

Viktor E. Frankl, "The Feeling of Meaninglessness: A Challenge to Psychotherapy," *American Journal of Psychoanalysis* 32, no. 1 (1972): 85-89.

Viktor E. Frankl, *The Unconscious God* (New York: Washington Square Press, 1975).

Viktor E. Frankl, "Paradoxical Intention and Dereflection," *Psychotherapy: Theory, Research & Practice* 12, no. 3 (1975): 226-237.

Viktor E. Frankl, "The Future of Logotherapy," *International Forum for Logotherapy* 4, no. 2 (1981): 71-78.

Viktor E. Frankl, *Man's Search for Meaning* (New York: Washington Square Press, 1984).

Viktor E. Frankl, *The Unheard Cry for Meaning: Psychotherapy and Humanism* (New York: Washington Square Press, 1984).

Viktor E. Frankl, *The Doctor and the Soul: From Psychotherapy to Logotherapy*, Revised and Expanded ed. (New York: Vintage Books, 1986).

Viktor E. Frankl, *The Will to Meaning: Foundations and Applications of Logotherapy* (New York: A Meridian Book, 1988).

Viktor E. Frankl, *Viktor Frankl's Recollections: An Autobiography* (New York: Plenum Press, 1997).

Viktor E. Frankl, *Man's Search for Ultimate Meaning* (New York: Plenum Press, 1997).

APPLICATIONS OF LOGOTHERAPY WITH AGED CLIENTS

Lawrence M. Brammer, "Counseling Theory and the Older Adult," *Counseling Psychologist* 12, no. 2 (1984): 29-37.

James C. Crumbaugh, "Aging and Adjustment: The Applicability of Logotherapy and the Purpose-in-Life Test," *The Gerontologist* 12, no. 4 (1972): 418-420.

Melvin A. Kimble, "Aging and the Search for Meaning," *Journal of Religion & Aging* Summer/Fall Vol. 6, no. 1/2 (1989).

Leo E. Missinne and Judy Willeke-Kay, "Reflections on the Meaning of Life in Older Age," *Journal of Religion & Aging* Summer Vol. 1, no. 4 (1985): 43-58.

Viktor Frankl Meets Karl Rahner:
Two Similar Anthropologies

R. Daren Erisman, MDiv

SUMMARY. The anthropology of Rahner, who is a German Jesuit priest, is similar to Viktor Frankl's anthropology. Both Rahner and Frankl are interested in the modern person and their difficulties. Rahner's categories of anthropology include humanity as person and subject, humanity as transcendent being, and humanity as responsible and free, while Frankl described the most fundamental aspect of being human as "will to meaning." This article explores the similarities and differences of Rahner and Frankl's anthropological categories, which arise from their own professional and religious perspectives. *[Article copies available for a fee from The Haworth Document Delivery Service: 1-800-342-9678. E-mail address: <getinfo@haworthpressinc.com> Website: <http://www.HaworthPress.com>]*

INTRODUCTION

I was reading a chapter from Karl Rahner's *Foundations of Christian Faith* when to my surprise I came upon the sentence:

Such a mystagogy, in which the individual person is made aware of the fact that this experience of transcendence really takes place repeatedly and without being called such in his immediate involvement with the concrete world, could be possible for the individual person only in individual conversation and in individual logotherapy.[1]

[Haworth co-indexing entry note]: "Viktor Frankl Meets Karl Rahner: Two Similar Anthropologies." Erisman, R. Daren. Co-published simultaneously in *Journal of Religious Gerontology* (The Haworth Pastoral Press, an imprint of The Haworth Press, Inc.) Vol. 11, No. 3/4, 2000, pp. 25-34; and: *Viktor Frankl's Contribution to Spirituality and Aging* (ed: Melvin A. Kimble) The Haworth Pastoral Press, an imprint of The Haworth Press, Inc., 2000, pp. 25-34. Single or multiple copies of this article are available for a fee from The Haworth Document Delivery Service [1-800-342-9678, 9:00 a.m. - 5:00 p.m. (EST). E-mail address: getinfo@haworthpressinc.com].

"Logotherapy!" I exclaimed to myself. It had been evident from my reading that Rahner was interested in similar categories of thought as Viktor Frankl and now in this one sentence my observation was confirmed. This sentence came amidst Rahner's discussion of transcendence and knowledge of God (subjects that Rahner was deeply involved in), and was part of a larger theme of anthropologic method. As I read further, I discovered that Rahner's anthropology was very similar to Viktor Frankl's anthropology and hence, the purpose of this paper came forthwith: To make a comparison of the anthropologies of Rahner and Frankl in order to enrich each other's "conversation" with our world.

Karl Rahner (1904-1984) is a capable theologian to make this comparison. As a German Jesuit priest who studied philosophy, notably under the existentialist philosopher Martin Heidegger, Rahner became a preeminent theologian of the Roman Catholic church. He was a professor of philosophy at the University of Munich and by the end of his life, his prolific writings totaled over 3,500 books and articles.[2] His notoriety especially grew during the Second Vatican Council held in Rome from 1962 to 1965 where he played a key role in bringing extensive changes to the church. His "mediating theology" took a middle ground between the extremes of integralism (the approach that seeks to keep the integrity of traditional Roman Catholic theology at any cost) and modernism (the approach that tries to make theology relevant to the modern mind to the point of being accommodating to secular culture). Rahner did this by interpreting what he saw as humankind's natural openness to the divine (Thomism) with modern transcendental philosophy.[3] Concisely, he conceived humans as innately reaching for the infinite (God) and thus grasping the finite (nature). The human spirit is, then, naturally transcendent, always seeking beyond itself because in God's grace humans were created that way. Humans reach towards the transcending Mystery of God and in doing so, truly understand their finite world as it exists in nature. His ideas and terminology still hold an important place within the Catholic tradition as well as Christianity as a whole.

Viktor Frankl (1905-1997), like Rahner, is a profound thinker. As an Austrian Jew, Frankl grew up with an interest in philosophy and after earning his Doctor of Medicine at the University of Vienna, he later completed his PhD in Philosophy there (he too was influenced by the philosophy of Heidegger). The founder of the School of Logotherapy, which later was called the Third Viennese School of Psychology (after Freud's psychoanalysis and Adler's individual psychology), Frankl made a significant impact on psychotherapy. He focused his attention on what he believed was most fundamental about being human: The will to meaning. Based on this human tendency for humans to desire meaning for their lives, he developed logotherapy as a way to facilitate this and bring healing to those who he thought were suffering from meaninglessness (what he calls an "existential vacuum").[4] His ideas were truly put to a test during World War II, when he survived three years of imprisonment in the concentration camps of Auschwitz and Dachau among others. He was a professor of neurology and psychiatry at the University of Vienna Medical School and his ideas and writings have influenced many in his field.

The structure of this paper flows out of Rahner's own categories of anthropology. They include: humanity as person and subject, humanity as transcendent being, and humanity as responsible and free. These categories fit Frankl's own categories extremely well and though there are definite differences, these differences come largely from their own professional and religious boundaries. As an inside note, I have chosen to use a more inclusive language than either Rahner or Frankl have observed. Therefore, I have substituted words such as "human" and "humanity" for Rahner and Frankl's more prevalent "Man."

HUMANITY AS PERSON AND SUBJECT

As one seeks commonality and differences between these two prolific thinkers, it is first of all evident that they are both interested in the modern person and their difficulties. Rahner describes this twentieth century person as being caught in an increasingly large and confusing body of world knowledge–knowledge that is both pluralistic in philosophy and religion. Interestingly, a colleague, Karl-Heinz Weger, describes Rahner's reflection on his own experience of modernity:

> Now, there are so many historical, metaphysical, philosophical, sociological, and religious problems that he (Rahner) confesses that he feels himself to be much more stupid than in the past, confronted with so much material available to the theologian.[5]

Rahner recognizes how the modern person struggles in the face of such a growing body of knowledge and accompanying pluralism. He also sees how it has led many into a crisis of faith. According to Rahner, as modern persons question the basic tenets of their faith in light of modernity, two issues have arisen: First, the question of the relationship of God's revelation of God's self in history. Second, the question of the relationship of God's revelation in a person's experience of themselves. It is in trying to answer these questions that Rahner begins his systematic approach to theology by using an anthropological approach and focusing first on the human as person and subject.

As person, each human is one who can understand and respond to God's message. They do this as a "whole" person and not just through some biological or psychological aspect. The fundamental reality then of the whole person, Rahner says, is the experience that humans become conscious of themselves and begin asking questions–questions that finally seek to go beyond the finite boundaries of sense perception into the transcendence of the infinite.[6]

Because it is individuals whose experiences shape their questioning, they cannot help but also be the "subject." There is therefore a subjective quality to the questioning which is unique to each individual. As they seek knowledge of the infinite, they discover something not only about what it means to be infinite but about what it means to be uniquely them. Here, then, Rahner's response to modernity's crisis of faith is met not with an abstract analysis of a distant God, but begins with the human as person and subject, relating his/her relationship with God with his/her own experience and understanding of himself/herself.

Though Frankl's emphases are different, he also responds to a crisis within modernity: the crisis of meaninglessness. For Frankl and his school of logotherapy, it is the will to meaning that is fundamental to being human and as people of the 21st century, he notes that people are apathetic in fulfilling this need, causing unnecessary hardship ("existential frustration") and even neuroses (what he calls "noogenic" neuroses).[7]

In responding to this crisis, Frankl, like Rahner, is interested in dealing with person as whole. In what Frankl calls "dimensional ontology" of humans, he relates the three dimensions: the somatic, the psychic, and the spiritual or "noological."[8] Though psychotherapy has historically dealt with the first two dimensions, Frankl declares, psychotherapy has not responded to the spiritual dimension, the third dimension. He continues by saying that this imbalance in treatment of the whole person has been a kind of psychologism within psychotherapy. He contends that he has solved the problem by emphasizing the unifying element of human nature, the spiritual dimension.[9] It is this spiritual dimension which Frankl uncovers in his existential analysis,

> To make the unifying image of man into a whole, a total image of true man, an image in all its dimensions, thus doing justice to that reality which belongs only to man and is called existence.[10]

Also akin to Rahner, Frankl views human nature as subjective. Frankl sees the subjective quality to human existence as humans try to seek meaning (like Rahner's emphasis on human questioning) because each person's seeking is determined by individual experience. This does not mean however that there is not an "objective" quality to this seeking. Meanings and values are not just self-expressions of an individual person but are found individually (subjectively) in reality. This provides both a subjective and objective quality to Frankl's thought.

Comparing Frankl's concept of existence and concern with the whole person, it certainly resembles Rahner's focus on the wholeness of a person as he reflects on a human's existential and transcendental nature. There is however an interesting point of difference between the two as Frankl is more hesitant to ascribe religion as being part of the "spiritual" dimension. Frankl recognizes the important place of religion when he discusses the conscience:

> Conscience has its 'still small voice' and 'speaks' to us–that is an undeniable psychological fact. What conscience says, however, is in every case a response. From the psychological point of view, the religious person is one who experiences not only what is spoken, but the speaker as well; that is, his hearing is sharper than the non-religious person's. In dialogue with his conscience– in this most intimate of possible monologues–his God is his interlocutor.[11]

But, Frankl does not want spiritual to simply mean religious. It seems to me that in Frankl's emphasis on having logotherapy applicable to every person, it is reasonable that Frankl would be cautious to make this distinction. Professionally, this allows him to treat the "non-religious" secular person as well as the "religious" person. Though

Rahner does not have quite the same problem since he is a professional theologian, Rahner too desires to communicate his message to non-religious people and some of Rahner's more generalizing, anthropologic talk may be a reflection of this.

HUMANITY AS TRANSCENDENT BEING

"Transcendence" is a key attribute of humans which both Rahner and Frankl recognize as essential to their respective anthropologies. For Rahner, transcendence, as discussed earlier, comes out of human questioning. Human experience is limited within a finite horizon of understanding, but our questioning takes us beyond this horizon to an unlimited one. Rahner claims this kind of questioning is built into persons and at one level, Rahner seems simply to be showing rational support for Augustine's claim that humans are created restless until they find their rest in God.[12]

Rahner supports Augustine's claim by using transcendental philosophy. He borrows from Kant, Maréchal and Heidegger to get the necessary pre-conditions for knowledge, and in the process proposes that there is an *a priori* transcendental condition built into humans that predisposes them to reflect beyond themselves. Unlike Kant, who limited this reflection to a horizontal horizon, Rahner takes such reflection to the vertical horizon of God. Finally, it is a human's natural reflection or perhaps better phrased, "openness" to God, which allows humans (unlike animals) to receive God's revelation and in the process grasp their own finitude, their own place as creatures of God.

Corresponding to this transcendental reflection by humans which reaches towards the infinite (but does not grasp it!), such reflection allows us to finally "know" finite reality as it truly is,[13] and to our dismay we also recognize our own mortality. Perhaps our anticipated death, more than anything, triggers such transcendental reflection and moves us beyond our apathy to recognize our experience as transcendental beings.

Frankl holds to a similar understanding as Rahner, that humans are transcendental beings, but Frankl phrases this more in terms of the human "will to meaning." This is at the heart of Frankl's anthropology and is what distinguishes his psychotherapy from Freud's emphasis on the human "will to pleasure" and Adler's emphasis on the human "will to power."[14] Such a will to meaning, declares Frankl, is in fact the primary motivation for the person:

> Man's search for meaning is the primary motivation in his life and not a 'secondary rationalization' of instinctual drives. This meaning is unique and specific in that it must and can be fulfilled by him alone; only then does it achieve a significance which will satisfy his own *will* to meaning [emphasis his]. There are some authors who contend that meanings and values are 'nothing but defense mechanisms, reaction formations and sublimations.' But as for myself, I would not be willing to live merely for the sake of my 'defense mechanisms,' nor would I be ready to die merely for the sake of my 'reaction formations.' Man, however, is able to live and even die for the sake of his ideals and values![15]

Frankl further describes this will to meaning as establishing a healthy tension that is essential for personal growth. This tension arises between two poles: The pole of a meaning to be fulfilled and the pole of the person who must fulfill it. Frankl calls such a tension "noodynamics," and he declares that it establishes a healthy tension between meaning and being.

Though Frankl believes that each person finds meaning unique to herself/himself, he declares that people in general find meaning in three ways: The first way is through creative work which we give to the world such as through our vocation, etc. The second way to finding meaning is experientially in what we get from the world such as through art and by the values experienced in nature and culture as well as through love. The third way is attitudinal and has, for example, to do with the ability to find meaning in the light of suffering.

Of these three categories of meaning, Frankl stresses the third attitude as being the most important because it is the one which must address the "tragic triad"[16] of human existence which is suffering, guilt and death. This triad makes people face their existence in a dramatic fashion. Whether someone is suffering from an incurable disease or is put into a concentration camp, or simply is reaching an elderly age, it is their attitude which shapes how they will experience their reality, and this is much of what logotherapy helps people to do: to help people find the meaning to their life situation, allowing them to grow in their attitude rather than fall into despair.

As one brings these similar ideas of transcendence of being together in these two thinkers, one might say that as Frankl advocates an *a priori* "will to meaning" in humans, Rahner similarly advocates an *a priori* "will to faith" in humans. Though Frankl would be hesitant to make these equivalent it seems possible that Rahner might be tempted to do so. Rahner's systematics would certainly benefit from Frankl's insights into humans and their need for meaning–a language that Rahner could use to speak effectively to non-Christians and the non-religious in general. Frankl, on the other hand, could use some of Rahner's conceptualizations to expand Frankl's own view of God which he touches on in his discussion of "super-meaning."[17] Frankl is not afraid to discuss religion or to use it as it is meaningful for "religious people," but Frankl largely focuses on the finite horizon of human activity for finding meaning rather than the abstract infinite horizon of God.

HUMANITY AS RESPONSIBLE AND FREE

As discussed in the earlier section on "humanity as person and subject," Rahner presumed that humans are able to understand and respond to the message of God. In making this presupposition, it follows then that humans also have freedom and therefore responsibility. This freedom and responsibility are transcendental in nature and have to do with "who one is as one creates oneself in time and relationships, the person one has already become, and the person one proposes to be in the future."[18] Though humans are entangled in a web of life circumstances, Rahner stresses that there is true freedom in our transcendence and that in this transcendence we are free to grow in knowing ourselves and to accept or reject God–hence, responsibility follows freedom.

Frankl too stresses the importance of human freedom and responsibility which he sees as coming out of the human spiritual dimension.[19] This freedom and responsibility make up the whole person and it is responsibility which is revealed by the conscience. Akin to Rahner, freedom and responsibility allow for a person to know themselves and as a side-effect of transcendence, to actualize themselves. Frankl emphatically points this out in his "categorical imperative" of logotherapy: "Live as if you were living already for the second time and as if you had acted the first time as wrongly as you are about to act now!"[20]

Frankl's understanding of freedom and responsibility are therefore similar to Rahner's understanding in that they both involve transcendence and a kind of actualizing of the self (though this is a side-effect and not the purpose).

CONCLUSION

Though I have only touched on three categories of Rahner and Frankl's anthropological method, it is clearly evident that they share much in common (strikingly so!) and it would be interesting to then compare how their anthropologies lead them into the worlds of Christianity and Judaism. Rahner has made a career out of extending his anthropology into extensive Christian theology, but Frankl has yet to push his anthropology with any depth into the realm of Jewish theology. Combining the two thinkers would provide an interesting PhD topic.

NOTES

1. Karl Rahner, *Foundations of Christian Faith: An Introduction to the Idea of Christianity*, trans. William V. Dych (New York: Crossroad, 1992), 59.

2. Stanley J. Grenz and Roger E. Olson, *20th Century Theology: God & the World in a Transitional Age* (Downers Grove, IL: InterVarsity Press, 1992), 240.

3. Carl E. Braaten and Robert W. Jenson, *A Map of Twentieth Century Theology: Readings from Karl Barth to Radical Pluralism* (Minneapolis: Fortress Press, 1995), 280.

4. Viktor E. Frankl, *Man's Search for Meaning: An Introduction to Logotherapy*, part of one trans. Ilse Lacsh (New York: Simon & Schuster, 1984), 111.

5. Karl-Heinz Weger, *Karl Rahner: An Introduction to His Theology* (New York: Seabury Press, 1980), 3.

6. Rahner, 30.

7. Frankl, *Man's Search for Meaning*, 106.

8. John J. Shea, "On the Place of Religion in the Thought of Viktor Frankl," *Journal of Psychology and Theology* 3 (Summer 1975): 179.

9. Viktor E. Frankl, "Religion and Existential Psychotherapy," *The Gordon Review* 6 (1960-61): 2.

10. Viktor E. Frankl, "Collective neuroses of the present day" in *Psychotherapy and Existentialism* (New York: Simon & Schuster, 1967) 130.

11. Viktor E. Frankl, *The Doctor and the Soul: From Psychotherapy to Logotherapy* (New York: Vintage Books, 1986), 62.

12. Grenz and Olson, 243.

13. Karl Rahner, *Hearers of the Word*, trans. Michael Richards (New York: Herder & Herder, 1969), 57.

14. Viktor E. Frankl, *The Will to Meaning: Foundations and Applications of Logotherapy*, trans. Richard and Clara Winston (New York: Penguin Books, 1988), viii.

15. Frankl, *Man's Search for Meaning*, 105.

16. Frankl, *The Will to Meaning*, 73.

17. Frankl, *Man's Search for Meaning*, 122.

18. Anne E. Carr, "Starting with the Human," a chapter from *A World of Grace: An Introduction to the Themes and Foundations of Karl Rahner's Theology*, edited by Leo J. O'Donovan (New York: Seabury Press, 1980), 24.

19. Shea, 179.

20. Frankl, *Man's Search for Meaning*, 114.

A Dialogue
Between Viktor Frankl and Charles Gerkin
Regarding the Living Human Document
and the Search for Meaning

Robert A. Rost, DMin

SUMMARY. This article briefly explores the connections between the thought of these two authors for the purpose of revealing the profound influence these men have on the principles and practice of geriatric pastoral care. This exploration is offered as a professional tribute by a pastor whose ministry with older adults is greatly enriched by their contributions. It is also offered as a personal testimony by a middle-aged individual whose own life journey is most encouraged and challenged by their thought. It is not every philosopher/psychiatrist or theologian/psychologist who can have such significant influence on both levels of the sojourner-in-ministry. Nor is it every author, whose insights are born of specific disciplines, who can offer such stimulating insights to those who are practitioners in another field. Both Viktor Frankl and Charles Gerkin possess these capabilities in abundance. The following "dialogue" simply serves as an invitation to partake of the wealth of their wisdom for both personal and professional enlightenment. *[Article copies available for a fee from The Haworth Document Delivery Service: 1-800-342-9678. E-mail address: <getinfo@haworthpressinc.com> Website: <http://www.HaworthPress.com>]*

Since Dr. Mel Kimble introduced me to the works of Viktor Frankl and Charles Gerkin, they have been two of the most profound in-

[Haworth co-indexing entry note]: "A Dialogue Between Viktor Frankl and Charles Gerkin Regarding the Living Human Document and the Search for Meaning." Rost, Robert A. Co-published simultaneously in *Journal of Religious Gerontology* (The Haworth Pastoral Press, an imprint of The Haworth Press, Inc.) Vol. 11, No. 3/4, 2000, pp. 35-42; and: *Viktor Frankl's Contribution to Spirituality and Aging* (ed: Melvin A. Kimble) The Haworth Pastoral Press, an imprint of The Haworth Press, Inc., 2000, pp. 35-42. Single or multiple copies of this article are available for a fee from The Haworth Document Delivery Service [1-800-342-9678, 9:00 a.m. - 5:00 p.m. (EST). E-mail address: getinfo@haworthpressinc.com].

35

fluences on both my principles and practice of geriatric pastoral care. So when he asked me to take part in the CARS conference on Dr. Frankl's contribution to the field of gerontology, it seemed natural for me to articulate how their dual influence shapes a vision of this ministry.

Both Frankl and Gerkin strongly uphold the primacy and dignity of the human person. Frankl perceives the person as a unique, indivisible unity which cannot be labeled nor split into or reduced down to component parts. Each person is spiritual and not just a psycho-somatic organism. The unconditional dignity of the person warrants unconditional reverence. Each person is existential, i.e., each person exists, not only as a factual being, but also in his or her potentialities and choices.[1] Gerkin, building on the work of Anton Boisen, writes that "each individual living human document has an integrity of his or her own that calls for understanding and interpretation, not categorization and stereotyping."[2] Psychologically speaking, the life of the self is a process of interpretation which takes shape in the person's story. Theologically speaking, the "life of the soul is a continuous life of interpretation,"[3] from the beginning to the end of life. From either perspective, such unending interpretation is the primary task of life.

Their complementary views on the human person shape their perceptions of the meaning of time. Frankl's existentialism asserts that the human person is constantly becoming and ever in process.[4] The transitoriness of human existence does not make life meaningless but rather "constitutes our responsibleness; for everything hinges upon our realizing the essentially transitory possibilities."[5] Human beings are not designed to exist in homeostasis, i.e., a tensionless state, but rather need to be "striving and struggling for a worthwhile goal, a freely chosen task."[6] Once a person has realized a value or fulfilled a meaning, he or she "has fulfilled it once and forever." "In the past, nothing is irrecoverably lost but everything irrevocably preserved and saved, safely delivered and deposited."[7] Frankl best exemplifies his positive outlook on the meaning of time in his image of the pages of a calendar which demonstrates the difference between the activist and the pessimist.[8] The activist focuses on the meanings fulfilled, while the pessimist sees only what little time is left. The image is an extremely relevant one for geriatric pastoral care because of the emphasis it places on values already realized and safe in "the surest kind of being." The image is also rather prophetic in a culture that both idealizes the endless possibilities of youth as well as employs selective amnesia about past achievements.

Gerkin actually develops an entire schema which depicts three levels of time: "time within the human life cycle, time within the process of human history, and time within the structure of the life of God in relation to creation–eschatological time."[9] The first level of time gives evidence that human becoming is "a continuous process of interpretation and reinterpretation" in which the "present moment of experience is always seen as in some sense an extension and continuation of the past."[10] The second level of time is where "we encounter the fact of human historical embeddedness" that acts as a boundary structure for any given human person.[11] Gerkin asserts that, in the third level of time, we discover our true and ultimate potential "within the purpose and promise of God."[12]

While this schema of three levels of time may be unique to Gerkin, I believe that the approach of Frankl's dimensional ontology, which he utilizes to comprehend both the unity and complexity of human existence, could be perceived as comparable.[13] Neither takes a simplistic nor negativistic view of time. Both promote the broadening and deepening of the search for meaning beyond immediate gratification or comprehension. Both condemn any sort of reductionistic approach to the human person as well as any attempt to define the person based on categories of power or determinism. They would hold that the striving to find meaning in one's life is the person's primary motivational force.

Frankl asserts that "this meaning is unique and specific in that it must and can be fulfilled by him alone; only then does it achieve a significance which will satisfy his own will to meaning."[14] He holds that meaning cannot be arbitrarily invented but conscientiously sought for and responsibly discovered. He defines conscience as the "intuitive capacity of man to find out the meaning of a situation." He contends that, in an era without normative values, human beings must "be equipped with the full capacity of conscience." He perceives the "foremost task of education is to refine that capacity which allows man to find unique meanings." Even the transitoriness of life and the fallibility of conscience does not dispense a person from responsible action. He says, "as Gordon Allport puts it, 'we can be at one and the same time half-sure and whole-hearted'."[15] In such development of conscience and striving for meaning, Frankl stresses self-transcendence. The "true meaning of life is to be discovered in the world rather than within man or his own psyche, as though it were a closed system." Becoming truly human means being directed to something or someone other than oneself, a meaning to fulfill or another person to encounter. "Self-actualization is possible only as a side-effect of self-transcendence."[16]

This would seem to be Frankl's primary ethical imperative–the responsibility to the unique meaning and purpose of one's life. Since such responsibility does not stop with retirement or the onset of the empty nest, Frankl's approach would have serious implications for geriatric pastoral care in an age of increasing longevity. It would seem that such ministry may well have an educational function of assisting those in or approaching later life with achieving the full capacity of conscience that can responsibly discern and actualize the true meaning of such longevity. Our ministry may also have a prophetic function of challenging and empowering our elders to continue to make contributions and form relationships by transcending their individual needs and desires.

Although Gerkin does not employ such explicitly ethical language, he would also disassociate himself from "psychotherapeutic norms for change based upon images of autonomy and individual self-actualization." He perceives such images of human potential and growth as "fundamentally idolatrous and alienating."[17] While he understands that "the road to authenticity is the road to integration of mutually disassociated aspects of the self," what is fully human "is not simply the wholism of the self and the overcoming of the self's fragmentation, but rather the wholism of an ecology of relationships." He holds that such self-transcendence is the ongoing work of divine incarnation and the activity of the Spirit.[18] Thus, for Gerkin, the educational and prophetic functions of pastoral care need to be grounded in the spiritual.

Frankl perceives this search for meaning as taking shape in three distinct groups of values. "The first is what he gives to the world in terms of his creations; the second is what he takes from the world in terms of encounters and experiences; and the third is the stand he takes to his predicament in case he must face a fate which he cannot change."[19] This second group of values refers to human relationships. He holds that each person establishes unity and completeness with a community, not within him or her self.[20] In love, human beings have the capacity to transcend themselves to grasp another in his or her innermost core, which holds not only the person's character but also his or her potential. "Furthermore, by his love, the loving person enables the beloved person to actualize these potentialities. By making him aware of what he can be and of what he should become, he makes these potentialities come true."[21] Ethically speaking, Frankl asserts that we are responsible for what we create, whom we love and how we suffer.[22] From my own experience, this perspective is very helpful for geriatric pastoral care precisely because it emphasizes personal responsibility in a comprehensive way that is applicable to all elders in any and all circumstances. It also emphasizes the responsibility of the pastoral caregiver to grasp the potential of the person in love and in community so as to encourage and enable the person to reach that potential.

Regarding Frankl's second group of values, Gerkin observes that one of the primary results of the process of pastoral counseling is that the person turns "away from primary concern for the self and its welfare toward concern for others." He would call this the process of appropriating one's "eschatological identity" in which the "self's pilgrimage, while uniquely and irrevocably personal, is joined with that larger pilgrimage of all persons, all aspects of existence." But such an identity cannot be sustained in a vacuum. "Only a community of shared vision and narrative structure can meaningfully sustain the level of continuing dialogue and shared experience that makes the continuation of a Christian life of pilgrimage possible."[23] Thus, pastoral care does not exist in a vacuum either. Rather, it is an integral and reciprocal part of the relationships and ministries of a community of faith living an eschatological mission.

Frankl holds that "attitudinal values are the highest possible values" and that "the meaning of suffering–unavoidable and inescapable suffering alone, of course–is the deepest possible meaning."[24] For, if there is meaning in the attitude one takes toward unavoidable suffering, then "life's meaning is an unconditional one."[25] Neither suffering nor dying can detract from it. Thus, "life never ceases to hold a meaning, for even a person who is deprived of both creative and experiential values is still challenged by a meaning to fulfill, that is, by the meaning inherent in an upright way of suffering."[26] But the ultimate meaning of human suffering cannot be grasped by the human intellect because it exists in a higher dimension than thought. What people need is "unconditional faith in unconditional meaning."[27] And it is Frankl's contention "that faith in the ultimate meaning is preceded by trust in an ultimate being, by trust in God."[28]

Frankl's treatment of the meaning of suffering as well as the necessity of faith and trust provides genuine validation for a significant portion of geriatric pastoral care. All of our care involves faith and trust on the part of everyone involved. Much of our care involves some unavoidable suffering and the perennial questions and dilemmas regarding the meanings hidden therein. Pastoral care, under these circumstances, is where the search for the unconditional takes place.

Gerkin's treatment of the meaning of suffering is strictly theological. "Suffering thus replaces power and omnipotence as the primary characteristic of God." In the event of the Cross, both Father and Son suffer in the act of abandonment. Now, for all time, Jesus "is to be sought wherever there is human suffering." He identifies with all who suffer and long for redemption. The Holy Spirit "is to be found wherever there is suffering in the not-yet-ness of the final unity of all things." The Spirit works in history as the "creator of a new future."[29] Such an insightful application of Trinitarian theology is most helpful to pastoral care in the Christian Tradition. It would be particularly relevant when the minister's careful listening to the person's search for meaning in the midst of suffering leads to appropriate prayer and ritual.

From this brief exposition of their respective treatments of the search for meaning in the midst of suffering one can readily see that, while Gerkin is both explicitly religious and Christian in his approach, Frankl keeps a firm boundary between his anthropology/psychotherapy and religion/theology. This is quite intentional on Frankl's part. He perceives that their "fusion confounds two different dimensions" of reality as well as two different goals, i.e., mental health and salvation. Frankl believes that it is the person "who has to decide whether he interprets responsibleness in terms of being responsible to humanity, society, conscience, or God. It is up to him to decide to what, to whom, and for what he is responsible."[30] Given both the pluralistic society and Church within which we offer pastoral care, Frankl's respect for the freedom of conscience of the individual in their struggles with their own suffering would be well to remember and even imitate.

When the interpretation of one's story and the search for meaning becomes painful or conflicted, especially in the midst of suffering, Gerkin perceives the need for the person to look "for a listener who is an expert at interpretation, one who can make sense out of what has threatened to become senseless."[31] From Frankl's point of view, such an expert does not take on the role of teacher or preacher. "To put it figuratively, the role played by a logotherapist is that of an eye specialist rather than that of a painter."[32] Such an expert enables and empowers persons to "see" for themselves the meanings of their own lives rather than scripting them with meanings from another source. This image of the "eye specialist" seems to be a rather apt and challenging one for the pastoral caregiver. It requires the minister to refrain from imposing his or her meanings on the other person, but, rather, to assist and accompany the person in his or her own search for meaning.

But, in order to live up to this requirement, Gerkin asserts that the minister must make his or her own "hermeneutical detour."[33] Since each of us is "embedded in our own historical process" and can never view ourselves from outside our history, each one must become "aware of one's own bias, so that the text may present itself in all its newness and thus be able to assert its own trust against one's own fore-meanings."[34] This is especially true since the therapeutic encounter requires "that both interpreter and the object of interpretation be changed at the fundamental level of meaning."[35] Such advice and admonition seems particularly relevant to geriatric pastoral care given the cultural conditioning to which we have all been subjected with regard to aging, loss, suffering and death. Unless we are constantly in the process of growing self-awareness, we cannot and, frankly, do not want to truly hear the stories of our elders and be changed in the encounters "at the fundamental level of meaning" within ourselves and within our communities.

As a pastor, I have tried to follow the advice and admonition of both Viktor Frankl and Charles Gerkin. I have found their insights enormously useful, not only for my geriatric pastoral care, but also for my own search for meaning. They have certainly helped me to put the mid-life issues of my own aging process in perspective as well as guide my ongoing hermeneutical detour toward a more enlightened self-awareness. Indeed, I have noticed that the more I actively and intentionally engaged in this process the better I can truly hear my elder parishioners and be changed by these encounters. I offer this personal testimony as I attempt to articulate the dialogue between them which is ongoing within my soul and throughout my ministry.

REFERENCES

1. Melvin Kimble's articulation of *Viktor Frankl's Ten Theses on the Human Person.*

2. Charles V. Gerkin, *The Living Human Document* (Nashville: Abingdon Press, 1984), p. 38.

3. Ibid., p. 104.

4. Kimble, *Frankl's Ten Theses on the Human Person.*

5. Viktor E. Frankl, *Man's Search for Meaning* (New York: Simon and Schuster, 1984), p. 124.

6. Ibid., p. 110.

7. Viktor E. Frankl, *The Will to Meaning* (New York: Penguin Books, 1988), p. 74.

8. Frankl, *Man's Search for Meaning*, pp. 124-125.

9. Gerkin, *The Living Human Document*, p. 105

10. Ibid., pp. 105 & 108.

11. Ibid., p. 110.

12. Ibid., p. 111.

13. Frankl, *The Will to Meaning*, pp. 22-26.

14. Frankl, *Man's Search for Meaning*, p. 105.

15. Frankl, *The Will to Meaning*, pp. 62-66.

16. Frankl, *Man's Search for Meaning*, p. 115.

17. Gerkin, *The Living Human Document*, p. 155.

18. Ibid., pp. 145-146.

19. Frankl, *The Will to Meaning*, p. 70.

20. Kimble, *Frankl's Ten Theses on the Human Person.*

21. Frankl, *Man's Search for Meaning*, p. 116.

22. Frankl, *The Will to Meaning*, p. 74.

23. Gerkin, *The Living Human Document*, pp. 179-189.

24. Frankl, *The Will to Meaning*, p. 75.

25. Frankl, *Man's Search for Meaning*, p. 118.

26. Frankl, *The Will to Meaning*, p. 70.

27. Ibid., p. 156.

28. Ibid., p. 145.

29. Gerkin, *The Living Human Document*, p. 67.

30. Frankl, *The Will to Meaning*, pp. 143-144.

31. Gerkin, *The Living Human Document*, p. 26.

32. Frankl, *Man's Search for Meaning*, p. 114.

33. Gerkin, *The Living Human Document*, p. 43.

34. Ibid., p. 45.

35. Ibid., p. 46.

Logotherapy and Pastoral Counseling

Melvin A. Kimble, PhD

SUMMARY. An intensive study of Frankl's logotherapy reveals its timely relevance for pastoral counseling. The paradigm of logotherapy recognizes the spiritual dimension as the inclusive and encompassing dimension for comprehending and integrating human phenomena. Its hermeneutical phenomenological analysis introduces an understanding of personhood which affirms one's capacity to find meaning in life, indeed, even in suffering and dying. It is this unique spiritual capacity which conveys a renewed awareness of self worth and human dignity and assists persons in understanding themselves as fashioned in the image of God. Logotherapy provides a helpful counseling theory for pastors and laity engaged in older adult ministry. *[Article copies available for a fee from The Haworth Document Delivery Service: 1-800-342-9678. E-mail address: <getinfo@haworthpressinc.com> Website: <http://www.HaworthPress.com>]*

I know what is wrong with me. It's metaphysical, not medical. I'm being reified, disincarnated and converted into an abstract. Everything human about me is atrophying.

Paddy Chayefsky, *The Latent Heterosexual*

No therapeutic theory can be developed without an implicit or explicit image of man.

Paul Tillich, *The Meaning of Health*

[Haworth co-indexing entry note]: "Logotherapy and Pastoral Counseling." Kimble, Melvin A. Co-published simultaneously in *Journal of Religious Gerontology* (The Haworth Pastoral Press, an imprint of The Haworth Press, Inc.) Vol. 11, No. 3/4, 2000, pp. 43-57; and: *Viktor Frankl's Contribution to Spirituality and Aging* (ed: Melvin A. Kimble) The Haworth Pastoral Press, an imprint of The Haworth Press, Inc., 2000, pp. 43-57. Single or multiple copies of this article are available for a fee from The Haworth Document Delivery Service [1-800-342-9678, 9:00 a.m. - 5:00 p.m. (EST). E-mail address: getinfo@haworthpressinc.com].

> Man lives by ideals and values. Human existence is not authentic
> unless it is lived in terms of self-transcendence.
>
> Viktor Frankl, *The Will to Meaning*

In spite of the facade of merriment and revelry and fervent hopes
for a fresh beginning that heralded the arrival of the new millennium,
the pervasive experience of "thingness" and a lifestyle of emptiness
continue to manifest themselves as the frightening descriptive syndrome of a planet inhabited, paradoxically, by *Homo sapiens*. This
blurring of the human image has created a mood of incomprehensibil-
ity concerning life and its meaning. Certainly no one dare deny that we
are living in an age that is confusingly complex and abounding in
bewildering and perplexing problems. On a personal level, they manifest themselves in the familiar themes of frustration and futility and
meaninglessness that make up so much of the emotional and intellectual climate of our time.

There is no lack of diagnoses, as well as descriptions of syndromes,
concerning the present ills of the world. Behavioral scientists have
been busily engaged in identifying and classifying the personal and
global maladies of our day. In an age influenced by a rodentomorphic
image of personhood as well as by a cybernetic ideology, we have
experienced the frightening diminishment of persons and the accompanying unconcern for their sanctity and worth. Biblical phrases such
as persons "being a little lower than the angels," for example, have a
hollow almost ludicrous ring in this technocratic age, with its life-con-
trolling, spirit-denying aspects. Max Frisch has suggested that technolo-
gy is the knack of so arranging the world that we need not experience
it.[1] All around us there seems to be grim evidence confirming the
observation made by Viktor Frankl, namely, that at first man viewed
himself as a creature fashioned after the image of his Creator. Then,
with the advent of the Industrial Age, man soon began to see himself
as the creator. And now, strange and sad to say, modern man has come
to see himself, Viktor Frankl suggests, after the image of his creation,
as a machine/computer.[2] This pervasive experience of *thingness* has
swept over our planet like a plague. The blurring and perverting of the
human image has resulted in the dehumanizing and depersonalizing of
our contemporary culture.

This is precisely why the addictive possibilities are so temptingly
attractive to so many in our society. They offer the promise of escape

from a reality that has become unbearably oppressive and lacking in meaning and fulfillment. Consequently, when "the therapy of the month" fails, there is an increasing number of persons, young and old, who ply themselves with combinations of chemicals that promise instant and blissful relief.

There is a desperately obvious need for an understanding of humankind that sets forth a person's capacity for self-transcendence. Frankl asserts, "When the self-transcendence of existence is denied, existence itself is distorted. It is reified. Being is reduced to a mere thing. Being human is depersonalized."[3]

Ironically, the unique characteristics inherent in the concept of self-transcendence (i.e., freedom and responsibility, decision and commitment, meanings and values, etc.) have been frequently overlooked or bypassed by those entrusted with the responsibility of treating humankind's spiritual malaise. In pursuit of "scientific objectivity," the psychotherapist and physician, and sometimes the pastor, have often been blind to the underlying philosophical and spiritual struggle of patients and counselees. Trained in theories and techniques which set forth mechanistic or rodentomorphic models of personhood, they are uncomfortable with and rejecting of intangible concepts which do not yield themselves to reductionistic explanation or quantitative measurements. This failure to recognize these integral transcendent human qualities magnifies the dehumanizing distortion of what it means to be human.

From the opaqueness of biomedical psychotherapeutic and health care models of personhood, Frankl's logotherapy emerges and clearly sets forth a multi-dimensional paradigm of personhood. With its hermenutical phenomenological methodology and insightful therapeutic principles concerning the essentials of human existence, logotherapy reclaims a wholistic model of human nature. It boldly and unapologetically introduces the indispensable intangibles of the noological dimension, and thereby corrects psychotherapy's reductionistic unidimensional view of personhood. Logotherapy rehumanizes psychotherapy.

Because logotherapy is concerned with more than simply the instinctual unconscious, its metaclinical tenets provide the therapist with understanding and insights with which to correct the lopsided plethora of nihilistic and reductionistic models of personhood. By aiming to bring persons to an awareness of responsibility in life and by emphasizing freedom to decide to whom and for what they are responsible, logotherapy restores human dignity and the matchless worth of the individual. As Frankl emphatically states:

> When a neurosis is noogenic, that is, when it has its roots not in psychological complexes and traumata but in spiritual problems, moral conflicts and existential crises, then such a spiritually rooted neurosis requires a psychotherapy focusing on the spirit.[4]

When practiced by a sensitive counselor and pastoral caregiver, the concepts of logotherapy become a powerful antidote to the diminishment of persons and the accompanying disregard for their sanctity and dignity. The phenomenon of self-transcendence is that which makes human beings *sui generis*, i.e., more than a closed system. Self-transcendence is what Frankl calls the "noological dimension," apart from which one is not fully human. It is because of the noological dimension of self-transcendence that any system of psychotherapy that seeks homeostasis or relief of tensions falls short. The noological dimension of the human being is the quality that allows a person to be more than a biological or psychological specimen.

A revised model of pastoral counseling for the 21st century urgently needs the corrective emphasis of logotherapy which goes beyond the narcissistic premise that individuals need nothing to affirm or satisfy but themselves. This Freudian picture of the self struggling to achieve equilibrium in the face of the imbalancing forces within remains a pathetic caricature of a person whose basic and authentic striving is to find and fulfill a meaning and who needs that noogenic tension which is the result of decision and commitment.

Gorden Allport objected to the homeostasis theory and stated that it "falls short of representing the nature of propriate striving whose characteristic feature is its resistance to equilibrium: tension is maintained rather than reduced."[5] Charlotte Buhler aired a similar critique concerning the homeostasis theory and its contention that creating values is a secondary goal and that all striving is for homeostasis satisfaction. She stresses the need to live with intentionality, which means living with purpose. The person has "a primary or native orientation, in the direction of creating and of values."[6]

One of Frankl's mentors, Rudolf Allers, pointedly focused on what had been overlooked by many counselors and psychotherapists: "The manner in which the psychiatrist conceives of his problem and his tasks, depends, whether he is aware of this or not, on the manner in which he conceives of human nature."[7] Pastoral counselors and psychotherapists had earnestly been trying to understand persons in their depths; now they need a new anthropological understanding of them in their heights. Frankl understood this well and, as early as 1938, described logotherapy as "height psychology."

> I thereby understand the primordial anthropological fact that being human is being always directed, and pointing, to something or someone other than one's self: to a meaning to fulfill or another human being to encounter, a cause to serve, for a person to love. Only the extent that someone is living out this self-transcendence of human existence, is he truly human or does he become his true self. He becomes so, not by concerning himself with his self's actualization, but by forgetting himself and giving himself, overlooking himself and focusing outward. Consider the eye, an analogy I am fond of evoking. When apart from looking in the mirror, does the eye see anything of itself? An eye with a cataract may see something like a cloud, which is its cataract; an eye with glaucoma may see its glaucoma as a rainbow halo around the lights. A healthy eye sees nothing of itself–it is self-transcendent.[8]

The tension between meaning and being cannot be eradicated. Frankl describes it by use of the imagery of the cloud of God's glory leading the Israelites through the desert:

> The meaning which a being has to fulfill is something beyond himself, it is never just himself. Only if this otherness is retained by meaning, can meaning exert upon a being that demand quality which yields itself to a phenomenological analysis of our experience of existence. Only a meaning which is not just an expression of being itself represents a true challenge. You remember the story in the Bible: When the Israelites wandered through the desert God's glory went before in the form of a cloud; only in this way was it possible for the Israelites to be guided by God. Imagine on the other hand, what would have happened if God's presence, the cloud, had dwelled in the midst of the Israelites; rather than leading them the right way, this cloud would have clouded everything, and the Israelites would have gone astray. In other words, meaning must not coincide with being; meaning must be

ahead of being. Meaning sets the pace for being. Existence falters unless it is lived in terms of transcendence toward something beyond itself.[9]

RESPONSIBLENESS—THE ESSENCE OF EXISTENCE

Responsibleness is the goal of a logotherapeutic transaction. For example, a patient is told by a logotherapist that responsibilities cannot be escaped, but can only be fulfilled. Logotherapy not only holds a mirror before the counselees as they view the unpleasant realities of their lives in the present, but it also educates them to see themselves as persons who are responsible for the way they shape their lives in the future. Because a person is seen in the nooetic dimension of being, responsibility is dealt with in its absolute depth—or height!

A logotherapeutic interview seeks to educate the persons toward being responsible. While the concept of responsibility reveals the character of life to be a task, at the same time this concept, like that of freedom, conveys hope. By bringing a personal capacity for responsibility before their consciousness, the logotherapist conveys to them that there is hope for self-directed change and improvement and that they, if they choose to be responsible, can re-shape their lives differently. Suddenly, they are confronted with the future, their future.

It should be pointed out that logotherapy does not threaten or moralize or impose the therapist's worldview (*Weltanschauung*) on the counselee. Instead, it appeals to the patient's capacity to be responsible and reaffirms freedom to be in control of one's life. Such an approach has the beneficial side effect of conveying a renewing awareness of self-worth and human dignity. The counselee's existential sovereignty over his or her life is reaffirmed.

By stressing that persons are not simply *homo machines* or psycho-somatic organisms, the counselor can counteract the crippling concept of psychologism which denies the defiant power of the human spirit and a person's capacity to be responsible. It is this sensitive awareness of one's unique spiritual capacity which helps to comprehend and appreciate oneself as fashioned *Imago Dei*. Pastoral counseling is enlarged and enriched by Frankl's statement that "logotherapy sees in responsibleness the very essence of human existence."[10]

On the one hand, the logotherapist helps the patients see that their lives are worth living and have meaning. On the other hand, a logotherapist like an optometrist assists counselees in bringing into focus the specific personal meanings and tasks that await fulfillment by them and them alone. Logotherapy punctures the psychotherapeutic fallacy that has caused counselors to be timid in raising questions concerning human destiny lest they violate some psychological code. Logotherapy does not avoid these questions. The logotherapist becomes a catalyst in assisting the counselee to detect and discover meanings and tasks awaiting completion.

The extent to which character is shaped and formed by the sufferings through which persons have endured is not determined by *what* has happened, but by the *response* and *attitude* towards what has occurred. A logotherapist does not minimize the sufferings of the counselee but rather challenges the person with the responsibility for integrating this suffering into one's present and future life. One's suffering is then "transmuted into a heroic and victorious achievement."[11] "A human being, by the very attitude he or she chooses, is capable of finding and fulfilling meaning in even a hopeless situation."[12]

Logotherapy's most unique contribution to this therapeutic interview is in assisting the counselee to become aware of responsibility for life. It does not focus on the past and use the distortions of the past to support an attitude of irresponsibility. Neither does it focus on the future in such a way as to breed some groundless hope or unrealistic illusion. Instead, it helps the person in redeeming the past by molding sufferings into something positive. It assists in understanding that the future need not be a fateful repetition of the past or the extension of the present suffering or void. To be free is to be free toward the future. The emphasis on responsibility in logotherapy brings hope because it believes that an individual has the freedom to alter and fashion his or her life and thereby the future. In a sense, it is one and the same thing to deprive a person of the future, or of hope. The deterministic models of personhood are guilty of doing exactly this. The concepts of freedom and responsibility are essential human characteristics, and individuals are deprived of the uniqueness of their humanity when they are ignored or violated.

Frankl provides an illuminating summary of meaning confrontation:

Once meaning orientation turns into meaning confrontation, that stage of maturation and development is reached in which freedom–that concept so much emphasized by existentialist philosophy–becomes responsibleness. Man is responsible for fulfillment of the specific meaning of his personal life. But he is also responsible *before* something, or *to* something, be it society, or humanity, or mankind, or his own conscience. However, there is a significant number of people who interpret their own existence not just in terms of being responsible to something but rather to *someone*, namely to God.

[In any case], logotherapy sees in responsibleness the very essence of human existence. Capitalizing on responsibleness to this extent, a logotherapist cannot spare his patient the decision for what and to what, or to whom, he feels responsible.[13]

In an earlier book, *Homo Patiens*, Frankl introduced this conviction very personally and forthrightly when he wrote:

Insofar as I exist, I exist spiritually and morally; insofar as I exist spiritually and morally, I exist with reference to meanings and values, I exist with reference to something that necessarily surpasses me in value, that is of an essentially higher order of value than my own being. In other words, I exist with reference to something that cannot really be a 'something' . . . but rather must be a 'someone' . . . or since it surpasses my person must be a supraperson. In short, insofar as I exist, I exist always with reference to God.[14]

Logotherapy's inclusion of a "supra-meaning" which describes life's unconditional meaningfulness and the ultimate meaning that embraces all of life further allows the pastoral counselor to erect their counseling model on logotherapeutic understanding of personhood that transcends individuals and their world.[15] Such a concept of a "supraperson" enables the pastoral counselors to be authentic and faithful to their own unique counseling faith orientation.

DEFIANT POWER OF THE HUMAN SPIRIT

One of logotherapy's most helpful contributions to counseling and pastoral care is its stress on the "defiant power of the human spirit."[16]

While fully recognizing the unity and the wholeness of a person, the logotherapist appeals to that which is above and beyond the person's somatic and psychic nature, namely, the spirit. The spiritual core of a person is capable of taking a stand not only toward negative and painful external circumstances and conditions, but also toward its own psychological character structure.

If persons regard themselves as overworked emotional mechanisms that simply need overhauling or a helpless brain machine that has no control over and responsibility for themselves, then, tragically, they have no capacity to transcend themselves or to fashion meaning from suffering.

From a theological perspective, Reinhold Niebuhr has helpfully described this concept of the defiant power of the human spirit as follows:

> Man is a child of nature, subject to its vicissitudes, compelled by its necessities, driven by its impulses, and confined within the brevity of the years which nature permits its varied organic forms, allowing them some, but not too much, latitude. The other less obvious fact is that man is a spirit who stands outside of nature, life, himself, his reason and the world.[17]

There is need to reemphasize this truth in contemporary counseling models.

THE AWARENESS OF POSSIBILITY

Logotherapy underscores the fact that persons are deciding beings. They exist as their own possibility! They have both actuality and potentiality. The freedom to choose and to change is ever present in a person's life, even in the last stage of the life cycle. While acknowledging the limiting circumstances and conditions that are ever present in a person's life, Frankl writes:

> Man is not fully conditioned and determined; he determines himself whether to give into conditions or stand up to them. In other words, man is ultimately self-determining. Man does not simply exist, but always decides what his existence will be, what he will become in the next moment.[18]

Niebuhr has written that "the essence of man is freedom."[19] Tillich has further elaborated concerning man's freedom:

> Man is essentially 'finite freedom'; freedom not in the sense of indeterminacy but in the sense of being able to determine himself through decisions in the center of his being. Man, as finite freedom, is free within the contingencies of his finitude. But within these limits he is asked to make of himself what he is supposed to become, to fulfill his destiny. In every act of moral self-affirmation man contributes to the fulfillment of his destiny, to the actualization of what he potentially is.[20]

The emphasis on the concept of freedom by Frankl and by such theologians as Tillich and Niebuhr needs to be listened to by pastoral caregivers less they "bless" the life-styles of self-pitying, choice-denying persons who seek them out for "counsel" and by so doing, re-inforce their counselee's experience of hopelessness and meaninglessness as they confront their present circumstances. The awareness of possibilities and the understanding that individuals are deciding beings convey hope. Hope must be seen in relationship to freedom. To be free is to stand before possibilities. It is to transcend the present situation and see one's capacity to alter the status quo, even if limited to one's own attitude toward unavoidable suffering. Without such a concept of freedom, there could be no hope. In an age influenced by a rodentomorphic image of personhood as well as by a cybernetic ideology, the concept of freedom needs to be re-emphasized in a pastoral care mode. Such persuasive statements concerning this unique capacity should be heeded by pastoral psychologists if they are to avoid the pitfall of a pan-deterministic counseling model. Frankl contends:

> Man is not 'driven', man decides. Man is free, but we prefer to speak of responsibility instead of freedom. Responsibility implies something for which we are responsible–namely, the accomplishment of concrete personal tasks and demands the realization of that unique and individual meaning which every one of us has to fulfill.[21]

ONTOLOGY OF TIME

A marked characteristic of logotherapy is that it takes time serious-ly. Its therapeutic thrust stresses the temporal nature of human exis-tence and the irreversible quality of human life. Although the logo-therapist does not play the game of psychic archeology nor engage in extensive Freudian subterranean excavations, neither is the past dis-missed as a "bucket of ashes." Rather, the counselee is accepted as one responsible for his or her personal life and the telling of it.

Memory implies time elapsed. In remembering an individual takes responsibility for values actualized and values denied. From time to time he must bear the pain of remembering himself as one who denied or negated values closely identified with his self-image. Memories of the past sometimes reflect and painfully recall unfulfilled self-expecta-tions. When potentialities are denied or left unfulfilled man experi-ences guilt. Not only are existential guilt and guilt feelings carried over from the past, but also the memory of certain positive and pur-poseful deeds and experiences and even the acceptance of avoidable suffering. Logotherapy's understanding of time is poignantly set forth by Frankl:

> The pessimist resembles a man who observes with fear and sad-ness that his wall calendar, from which he daily tears a sheet, grows thinner with each passing day. On the other hand, the person who attacks the problems of life actively is like a man who removes each successive leaf from his calendar and files it neatly and carefully away with its predecessors, after first having jotted down a few diary notes on the back. He can reflect with pride and joy on all the richness set down in these notes, on all the life he has already lived to the full. What will it matter to him if he notices that he is growing old? Has he any reason to envy the young people he sees, or wax nostalgic over his own lost youth? What reasons has he to envy a young person? For the possibilities open to a young person, the future that is in store for him? "No, thank you," he will think, "Instead of possibilities, I have realities in my past, not only the reality of work done and of love loved, but of sufferings bravely suffered. These sufferings are the things of which I am most proud, though these are things which cannot inspire envy."[22]

In logotherapy even the anxiety of death itself becomes a positive factor in an existential synthesis which focuses on individuals' responsibility:

> For man resembles a sculptor who chisels and hammers the unshaped stone so that the material takes on more and more form. Man works the matter with which fate has supplied him: now creating, now experiencing or suffering, he attempts to 'hammer out' values in his life–as many as he can of creative or experiential or attitudinal values.

> We can also introduce the factor of time into this simile of the sculptor: we need only imagine that the sculptor has a limited span of time at his disposal for completing his work of art–but that he is not informed when his deadline is. Thus he never knows when he is going to be 'called away,' whether the summons may not come in the very next minute. He is therefore forced to use his time well in any case–lest his work remain abortive. That time runs out before the work is completed by no means makes it worthless, however.[23]

The pastoral counselor can integrate logotherapy's emphasis that time matters and needs to be dealt with responsibly with other insights concerning the mystery of time and its potential for meaning fulfillment.

THE PSYCHOTHERAPEUTIC RELATIONSHIP

Frankl has suggested that the equation $\Psi = x + y$ points to the fact that "the crucial agency in psychotherapy is not so much the method, but rather the relationship between the patient and doctor or . . . the 'encounter' between the therapist and patient."[24] Pastoral counselors need this understanding of the therapeutic relationship. To counsel troubled parishioners is more than to apply a technique as if they were simply overworked emotional mechanisms, but it is to confront with possibilities and to challenge toward decisive action in life. For such challenges to be accepted, the therapeutic encounter must not be simply between counselor and counselee, but between two human beings " . . . of which one confronts the other with logos, that is, the meaning of being."[25]

Pastoral care needs the corrective emphasis of the concepts of logotherapy which "stiffnecks" (to use Frankl's own descriptive phrase) pastoral counselors to overcome their strange reluctance to confront the *humanitas* of the *homo patiens* and encourage a personal encounter concerning meanings and values. In a pastoral counseling relationship, the counselees need to feel free to plumb the depths of their spirits and to probe and examine, sometimes in a needful agonizing manner, what there is that justifies *not* taking their life or that encourages them to continue struggling with negative circumstances and forces around them. The therapist then facilitates the despairing person in gathering up the fragments of life and helps to create a new awareness of one's life situation.

Logotherapy recognizes that no one gets well or becomes whole on the couch or chair in the office of a psychotherapist or pastoral counselor. Persons only get well in the arena of life. By its appellative approach to meaning to be fulfilled in life, logotherapy embraces the dimensions of being in such a way that they are brought together in a dynamic synthesis that gives persons an understanding of themselves drawn with the bold lines of realism and hope. It assists them in interpreting their present predicament and examining possibilities for the future and paths for responsible actions in moving toward that future. It gives persons awareness of their spiritual capacities and an ultimate understanding of living as *sub specie aeternitatis*. By so doing, logotherapy leaves the door open to the unique specialized role and faith orientation of the pastoral caregiver.

The risk is always present in any counseling relationship that the counselor will fail to grasp the existential problem and predicament of the counselee. Similarly, there is always the real possibility that the counselee will irresponsibly choose or decide what is detrimental and destructive to his or her spiritual life. Obviously, no therapeutic relationship can force persons to be responsible for becoming what they have the potential to become.

Certainly the words of the prophet are as true today as when they were written some 2500 years ago; "the heart of man is a stubborn thing and full of fears" (Jeremiah 17:9). But as the logotherapist participates with the counselees in their struggle to become aware of the possibilities and necessities of life and to accept responsibility for fulfilling the meaning of their lives, they will be made wonderfully aware that this same finite creature has indeed been marvelously fashioned, not as a machine, but in the words of the psalmist, "a little lower than the angels" (Psalm 8:5).

CONCLUSION

Pastoral caregivers, like psychotherapists, have the inescapable challenge in this technotronic age to try to bring healing and wholeness to despairing persons plagued with the brooding sense of an existential vacuum and meaninglessness which characterizes the sickness of our times (*krankheit des zeitgeistes*). Logotherapy provides pastoral caregivers with insights into this task and beckons to them from the boundary-line of medicine to share in this helping ministry. The pastoral counselor will surely welcome this invitation, for in this secular age they have sometimes become uncertain about their unique therapeutic role.

The logotherapeutic tenet that self-transcendence is the essence of existence opens the door to a deeper understanding of a person's capacity to be dedicated and devoted to something beyond oneself. By its concept of dimensional ontology, logotherapy provides pastoral care givers with a creative interpretation of the ontological differences and anthropological unity of personhood. By describing the noological dimension from the perspective of descriptive hermeneutical phenomenological analysis, it enriches the pastor's understanding of meanings and values, of freedom and responsibility, of conscience and commitment, of decision and responsibleness, of suffering and faith, of love and work. Logotherapy exegetes what Reinhold Niebuhr has characterized as "the basic question of religion," namely, "the problem of meaning."[26] It dynamically focuses on what Tillich pointed to when he wrote: "Man is ultimately concerned about his being and his meaning."[27]

Because logotherapy affirms that persons need an unconditional faith in unconditional meaning and because it boldly follows them into the labyrinthine depths of the spiritual dimension of their being, it is the uniquely therapeutic theory to enlarge and inform pastoral counseling with older adults. The principles of logotherapy assist pastoral counselors in blending their theological understanding with their knowledge of the human psyche in such a dynamically creative manner that they are better able to steer a responsible course between the Scylla of theologism and the Charybdis of psychologism.

NOTES

1. Max Frisch, *Homo Faber* (San Diego: Harcourt Brace, 1987).

2. Lecture presented by Viktor Frankl at Luther Seminary. May, 1972.

3. Viktor Frankl, *The Unheard Cry for Meaning: Psychotherapy and Humanism* (New York: A Touchstone Book, 1978), 53.

4. Ibid.

5. Gordon Allport, *Becoming: Basic Considerations for a Psychology of Personality* (New Haven, Connecticut: Harper and Brothers, 1955), 49.

6. Charlotte Buhler, "Some Observations on the Psychology of the Third Force," *Journal of Humanistic Psychology,* 5 (1965) 54.

7. Rudolf Allers, *Existentialism and Psychiatry* (Springfield, Illinois: Charles C. Thomas Publishers, 1961) 4.

8. Viktor Frankl, *The Unheard Cry for Meaning,* 35.

9. Frankl, *Psychotherapy and Existentialism* (New York: Washington Square Press, 1967) 11-12.

10. Frankl, *Psychotherapy and Existentialism,* 13.

11. Ibid., 90.

12. Frankl, *The Will to Meaning* (New York: World Publishing Co., 1969) 75.

13. Frankl, *Psychotherapy and Existentialism,* 12-13.

14. Frankl, *Homo Patiens* (Wien: Verlag Franz Deuticke, 1950), 69.

15. Frankl, *Psychotherapy and Existentialism,* 57

16. Ibid., 99.

17. Reinhold Niebuhr, *The Nature and Destiny of Man* (New York: Charles Scribner and Sons, 1943) 3.

18. Frankl, *Man's Search for Meaning* (New York: Touchstone Book: Simon & Schuster, 1978), 206.

19. Niebuhr, 17.

20. Paul Tillich, *The Courage to Be* (New Haven: Yale University Press, 1952), 52.

21. Frankl, *Psychotherapy and Existentialism,* 127.

22. Frankl, *The Unheard Cry for Meaning,* 104-105.

23. Frankl, *The Doctor and the Soul* (New York: Alfred A Knopf, 1957), 74-75.

24. Frankl, *Psychotherapy and Existentialism,* 144.

25. Frankl, *The Will to Meaning,* 9.

26. Niebuhr, 164.

27. Paul Tillich, *Systematic Theology* vol. 1. (Chicago: University of Chicago Press, 1951), 14.

The Similarities
Between Frankl's Logotherapy
and Luther's Concepts of Vocation
and the Theology of the Cross

Scott C. Peterson, MDiv

SUMMARY. This paper focuses on the similarities between Viktor Frankl's Logotherapy and Martin Luther's concepts of Vocation and the Theology of the Cross. The search for meaning for Frankl finds its expression in the vocation toward the neighbor of Luther. It is this relationship with the neighbor which provides both the arena for becoming a self and also for finding meaning in the outreach to the neighbor. The subject of suffering and the "tragic triad" also has relationships with Luther's theology of the cross in its movement through suffering to meaning. *[Article copies available for a fee from The Haworth Document Delivery Service: 1-800-342-9678. E-mail address: <getinfo@haworthpressinc.com> Website: <http://www.HaworthPress.com>]*

How are we to see life? Is it an existence of meaningless movement from one minute to the next, one day to the next; or is there a higher purpose in life, something for which we are able to look forward and for which we strive?

Soren Kierkegaard is known as the "Father of Existentialism" and asked this question as well. He posited also the question of whether existence comes before essence or vice versa. Or in other terms, where we "are" or "have being" before we "are something or someone" or

---

[Haworth co-indexing entry note]: "The Similarities Between Frankl's Logotherapy and Luther's Concepts of Vocation and the Theology of the Cross." Peterson, Scott C. Co-published simultaneously in *Journal of Religious Gerontology* (The Haworth Pastoral Press, an imprint of The Haworth Press, Inc.) Vol. 11, No. 3/4, 2000, pp. 59-66; and: *Viktor Frankl's Contribution to Spirituality and Aging* (ed: Melvin A. Kimble) The Haworth Pastoral Press, an imprint of The Haworth Press, Inc., 2000, pp. 59-66. Single or multiple copies of this article are available for a fee from The Haworth Document Delivery Service [1-800-342-9678, 9:00 a.m. - 5:00 p.m. (EST). E-mail address: getinfo@haworthpressinc.com].

whether this being "something or someone" is a necessity before we "are." This question still is asked by many today and the search for meaning in one's existence beyond "who" or "what" we are, and also beyond the suffering that surrounds us, utilizes much energy in our lives. Kierkegaard also understood this suffering in life and this feeling of meaninglessness which if unchecked leads to despair. For Kierkegaard this despair becomes what he defines as the "sickness unto death," for it is only this deep despair of suffering without meaning that can destroy our being.[1] But how do we move beyond this meaninglessness and despair? How do we live a life that seems to have no meaning and only contains suffering? These have been the questions that have been approached by two different modes of thought, one being the philosophical/religious and the other being the psychological. Each of these has been seen to be separated from the other as the definition of "what" or "who" a person's existence is, as well as how to relate to this person, this "being." This paper engages the task of looking at the work of Viktor Frankl and his psychological approach in light of Martin Luther's concept of the theology of the cross. An attempt is made to show that the psychological and philosophical/religious modes of thought can be complementary and even support one another in their endeavor to search for meaning in life.

FRANKL'S LOGOTHERAPY

Let us begin first with the work and thought of Viktor Frankl and his concept of logotherapy. As I have written above about the existentialism of Kierkegaard and the questions he raises, so also must we understand the foundation of Frankl's thought and his logotherapy. Frankl was influenced by other existentialist philosophers, namely Husserl and Heidegger, and their concepts and ideas of the existence of the human person. Beginning with the "being" of a person in opposition to "what" or "who" a person is, moves the question of existence within a person and to the "is" of a person instead of the outer nature or essence of a person. A person gains meaning because he or she is, not because he or she is "something." This concept fueled Frankl's ideas of the meaning grasped by a person when all else had been taken from her or him.

In his book *Man's Search for Meaning,*[2] Frankl writes about his experiences in World War II prison camps and his observations as to how persons dealt with this new existence where everything they had been and known was taken from them and they had only themselves. They were lowered to the basics of "being" and it was here that they searched for meaning. For Frankl this search for meaning was observed as a "prime motivational force in man"[3] and became imperative in the fight for survival in the prison camps. Frankl focused on the "will to meaning" in opposition to Freud's "pleasure principle" or as Frankl puts it, the *will to pleasure*, and to the Adlerian focus on "striving for superiority," coined as the *will to power*. These two approaches become meaningless in the setting of the prison camps as there was no pleasure to be found as well as no power to be gained. This search for meaning must come from within a person and a person's existence alone when all other has been taken.

For Frankl the human person and human existence always point to something other. This existence of being human has three elements: (1) the freedom of the will, the ability to make choices in reference to his or her existence; (2) the will to meaning, or the search for that which gives meaning; and (3) the meaning of life, which must be objective and not merely subjective.[4] It is these three which work together in that search for meaning in life. In this focus on something other Frankl quotes Nietzsche where he says, "He who has a *why* to live for can bear almost any *how*."[5] It is this "why," this meaning in life, which gives life an impetus to work toward survival and to find meaning in even the most horrendous places and situations. Thus, human existence is not to be one of a tensionless being, but "what man actually needs is not a tensionless state but rather the striving and struggling for a worthwhile goal, a freely chosen task. What he needs is not the discharge of tension at any cost but the call of a potential meaning waiting to be fulfilled by him. What man needs is not homeostasis but what I call 'noo-dynamics,' e.g., the existential dynamics in a polar field of tension where one pole is represented by a meaning that is to be fulfilled and the other pole by the man who has to fulfill it."[6] This tension is that which gives the impetus to continue the fight for survival when all seems lost. When this meaning is not seen or known these persons are caught in the state which Frankl calls the "existential vacuum."[7] This "existential vacuum" manifests itself as boredom and this boredom encompasses the whole of a person's existence to where nothing else can be seen. It is within this state where a person can no longer see the "other" and so does not see a meaning in life. But how does one come to know what this meaning is?

"One should not search for an abstract meaning of life. Everyone has his own specific vocation or mission in life to carry out a concrete assignment which demands fulfillment. Therein he cannot be replaced, nor can his life be repeated. Thus, everyone's task is unique as is his specific opportunity to implement it."[8] This meaning in life is individual, but is not subjective. This meaning has objective reality outside the person as it comes into contact with the "other." This meaning is found in the situation of "being responsible." Frankl writes, "This emphasis on responsibleness is reflected in the categorical imperative of logotherapy, which is: 'Live as if you were living already for the second time and as if you had acted the first time as wrongly as you are about to act now!'" It is in being responsible that one finds meaning in life, but it is in this awareness of his or her own responsibleness where one must be free to choose for what, to what, or to whom he or she is responsible.[9] In this responsibleness a person finds it necessary to be in relationship with an "other" and in this responsibleness toward this "other" a person finds meaning not in the search for self-actualization, but rather in giving herself or himself to this "other." It is in this movement toward the other that the person becomes most human and is actualized.[10]

LUTHER'S CONCEPT OF VOCATION AND THE THEOLOGY OF THE CROSS

For Frankl this meaning in life can be discovered "in three different ways: (1) by creating a work or doing a deed; (2) by experiencing something or encountering someone; and (3) by the attitude we take toward unavoidable suffering."[11] The first of these two has relevance to Martin Luther's concept of vocation, and the neighbor and the third with Luther's Theology of the Cross.

For Luther the importance of the neighbor was paramount to living on this earth from day to day. Daily life was not to be spent reaching upward toward heaven to assure salvation, for we could do nothing in working toward our being saved; that was the work of Christ. But our lives were to be spent reaching out to our neighbor who was in need and helping to fulfill those needs. In service to the neighbor, the Christian lives the "true" life of the Christian, for that is where we can make a difference. This is the "vocation" of the Christian–to work in the lives of his or her neighbors, providing help and assistance in all times and situations. In this earthly realm is where vocation happens, and this vocation involves the neighbor as the recipient of our action. This neighbor may be a co-worker, a person who lives nearby, a brother or sister, mother or father, or even the stranger we meet on the road. It is our different relationships with these persons that will guide how our vocation will be best lived out. We would not have the same vocation in relation to the stranger that we would have in relation to our children; each is different and unique. All of our relationships call upon us to enter into a vocation in response to that relationship.

It is the vocation of the Christian to live a life in relationship with the neighbor which emerges out of a relationship with God. It is in the daily tasks that one lives out that faith which has been given, as well as continually experiencing new parts of that faith. It is in this faith and in one's work toward the neighbor that we find that meaning which gives us strength. Of all one has explored, one thing is the same: the human person. All this discussion is about humankind in the relationship with the neighbor. It is with this world that a person is concerned, for it is in this world that we live and act. But a person does not find oneself without problems in this life, as Gustaf Wingren states in his book *Luther on Vocation,* "Luther's concept of the world and his view of life are characterized by the dualism between God and Satan on the one hand, and on the other, eschatology or the tension between earth and heaven."[12] The human is caught in tension between poles, and in this tension and struggle is life lived. The human person has a special place in creation, as "of all earthly things it is only man whose objective is heaven. And of all earthly creatures it is man who is the object of the struggle between God and Satan."[13] In this place humans often experience their vocation as imitation of Christ, but, "Luther places vocation in sharp contrast with imitation,"[14] as, "Christ is not to be imitated by us, but rather to be accepted in faith, because Christ also had his special office for the salvation of man, an office which no one else has."[15] Christ's office is one that humans are not able to imitate, for it is a cosmological office, and humans are but here in the earthly realm; it is to the neighbor that one is called. This is the office of the human, and in this office we are called to *all* of our neighbors.

Thus it is in creating a work or doing a deed in encountering the neighbor where one becomes fully human and where one finds meaning. We are always presented with the opportunity to enter into relationship with the neighbor and it is in this endless opportunity that one finds the strength to go on as one reaches out to the other. But there is also meaning to be found in the attitude we take in relation to the unavoidable suffering in life. It is the attitude toward this suffering which moves us through seeing suffering as meaningless and haphazard toward a purposeful outlook within our suffering. For Frankl "suffering ceases to be suffering at the moment it finds a meaning, such as the meaning of sacrifice."[16] For if we remember, "It is one of the basic tenets of logotherapy that man's main concern is not to gain pleasure or to avoid pain but rather to see a meaning in his life. That is why man is ever ready to suffer, on the condition, to be sure, that his suffering has a meaning."[17]

In Luther's "Heidelberg Disputation," he writes, "A theologian of glory calls evil good and good evil. A theologian of the cross calls the thing what it actually is."[18] It is here that the theologian of the cross sees suffering as suffering, but also sees within the suffering the hidden God. For what is to be said of Jesus' suffering and death on the cross if within the cross there is no meaning? Jesus' death would be just one more death if God was not hidden in the death and suffering, and through that presence give meaning, even ultimate meaning, to the cross. Luther continues in his explanation, "God can be found only in suffering and the cross," and also, "It is impossible for a person not to be puffed up by his good works unless he has first been deflated and destroyed by suffering and evil until he knows that he is worthless and that his works are not his but God's."[19] Here one sees again Frankl's concept of self-actualization only happening when one forgets oneself and focuses on the other.

As one searches for the meaning in suffering one moves beyond himself or herself and looks toward the neighbor; in this we know the relationship of vocation. One finds meaning in relationships outside of oneself, with spouse or children, friends and colleagues, and with God. It is in these relationships and others that one sees that which is greater than even the suffering one experiences and one is able to move through suffering to meaning. For Frankl human existence is portrayed within what he calls the "tragic triad."[20] This triad consists of pain, guilt, and death. Each of these has a great part in the life of the human and cannot be avoided. But can one find hope and meaning even in the face of these factors? Frankl contends that there is within this "tragic triad" an even more powerful "tragic optimism" which works itself out in three ways in relation to the tragic triad: (1) by turning suffering into a human achievement and accomplishment; (2) by deriving from guilt the opportunity to change oneself to the better; and (3) by deriving from life's transitoriness an incentive to take responsible action.[21] In each of these it is the movement from the situation to finding meaning in the situation which brings optimism and strength.

CONCLUSION

Having entered into a dialogue between Frankl and Luther one observes similarities between them. For both, responsibility to the neighbor and meaning in suffering give a person a "why" to live. It is in living for something greater, something other, than we ourselves which gives meaning to life. One's existence is a movement from 'being' to 'being in' and 'being for' something other, and it is in this movement that meaning is discovered which brings life, hope, and strength. Meaning is found not in the abstract, but in the particular. It is in one's relationships with those around us that meaning is to be found, so that even in the midst of suffering it is necessary that one continues in an 'office' or 'vocation' to which one has been called. We move past pain, guilt, and death and enter an existence of relationship where it is the particular that gives meaning.

NOTES

1. Soren Kierkegaard, *The Sickness Unto Death: A Christian Psychological Expostion for Upbuilding and Awakening.* Trans. by Howard V. Hong and Edna H. Hong. (Princeton, NJ: Princeton University Press, 1980).
2. Viktor E. Frankl, *Man's Search for Meaning.* Third Edition. Trans. by Ilse Lasch. (New York: Simon & Schuster, 1984).
3. Ibid., 104.
4. Melvin A. Kimble, Lecture on "Aging and the Search for Meaning," delivered at Luther Seminary, St. Paul, Minnesota, April 29, 1996.
5. Frankl, 109.
6. Ibid., 110.
7. Ibid., 111.
8. Ibid., 113.
9. Ibid., 114.

10. Ibid., 115.

11. Ibid.

12. Gustaf Wingren, *Luther on Vocation*. Trans. by Carl C. Rasmussen. (Philadelphia, PA: Muhlenberg Press, 1957), 162.

13. Ibid., 163.

14. Ibid., 171.

15. Ibid., 172.

16. Frankl, 117.

17. Ibid.

18. Martin Luther, "Heidelberg Disputation." *Martin Luther's Basic Theological Writings*. Ed. Timothy F. Lull. (Minneapolis, MN: Fortress Press, 1989), 31.

19. Ibid., 44.

20. Frankl, 139.

21. Ibid., 140.

Actions, Feelings, and Values: Foundations of Meaning and Personhood in Dementia

Susan H. McFadden, PhD
Mandy Ingram, BS
Carla Baldauf, BS

SUMMARY. Viktor Frankl's writings on the sources of meaning in human life are compared to emergent views on personhood in older individuals with dementing illnesses. An ethnomethodological study of a CBRF (community based residential facility) with two sections, each housing about 10 persons, revealed meaning in residents' actions, feelings, and expressions of values. These individuals showed it is possible to retain what Frankl called "tragic optimism" despite cognitive deterioration. Through active engagement with their environments and with one another, a wide range of expressed emotions including happiness and humor, and caring sensitivity toward others, these elders showed that given a supportive environment, dementia does not destroy meaning. These observations form the basis of suggestions for pastoral care and ministry with people with dementia. *[Article copies available for a fee from The Haworth Document Delivery Service: 1-800-342-9678. E-mail address: <getinfo@haworthpressinc.com> Website: <http://www.HaworthPress.com>]*

Susan H. McFadden is Professor of Psychology at the University of Wisconsin Oshkosh, Oshkosh, WI 54901. Mandy Ingram is employed with the Wisconsin State Corrections Board. Carla Baldauf is an MSW candidate at the University of Wisconsin Milwaukee.

[Haworth co-indexing entry note]: "Actions, Feelings, and Values: Foundations of Meaning and Personhood in Dementia." McFadden, Susan H., Mandy Ingram, and Carla Baldauf. Co-published simultaneously in *Journal of Religious Gerontology* (The Haworth Pastoral Press, an imprint of The Haworth Press, Inc.) Vol. 11, No. 3/4, 2000, pp. 67-86; and: *Viktor Frankl's Contribution to Spirituality and Aging* (ed: Melvin A. Kimble) The Haworth Pastoral Press, an imprint of The Haworth Press, Inc., 2000, pp. 67-86. Single or multiple copies of this article are available for a fee from The Haworth Document Delivery Service [1-800-342-9678, 9:00 a.m. - 5:00 p.m. (EST). E-mail address: getinfo@haworthpressinc.com].

INTRODUCTION

Viktor Frankl's wholistic view of humanity and his descriptions of the ways meaning is discovered and experienced are consistent with an emerging new perspective on dementia. Inspired by the work of British psychologist Tom Kitwood,[1,2] social workers, psychologists, chaplains, nurses, and long term care administrators around the country are calling for radical changes in the present culture of care of persons with Alzheimer's disease and other dementing illnesses of old age. Images of a new culture of care convey Kitwood's conviction that dementia is a disability. Just as we do not assume the paralyzed, deaf, or blind person has lost personhood, neither should we believe that the individual whose brain is accumulating neuritic plaques and tangles has lost his or her essential humanity. Such a perspective on one of our times' most frightening illnesses would undoubtedly be applauded by Viktor Frankl.

Alzheimer's disease, the most common form of progressive, degenerative dementing illnesses, currently affects about 4 million Americans. Given the demographic trends of an aging society, the projected number of persons suffering from Alzheimer's will rise to 14 million Americans by 2050. Current estimates are that about 10% of persons 65 and older suffer from Alzheimer's and that nearly 50% of individuals 85 and older have this disease. Approximately 70% live at home and are cared for by family members, most often a spouse or adult daughter.[3]

Although considerable research has been conducted on the neurobiology of dementia, so far no definitive cause or cure has been identified. Much research has also been directed toward charting decline and defining discrete stages of this progressive illness in an effort not only to conduct better diagnostic evaluations, but also to design appropriate care responses. Another major aspect of research on dementia concerns caregiver stress. Psychologists' research efforts have been largely directed at describing the nature and effects of the cognitive losses and at differentiating dementia, depression, and delirium.

A number of significant issues have not attracted the amount of research attention they deserve. For example, greater understanding is needed of the ways this illness is socially constructed. The fears experienced by aging persons who forget where they placed their glasses or who cannot recall an acquaintance's name contribute to definitions of the illness just as much as scientific descriptions of changes in neural structure and function. In a society so proud of its vast abilities to generate and store information, the threat of losses of cognitive capacity in the human brain takes on enormous social significance. By favoring a strictly biomedical approach to Alzheimer's and other dementing illnesses, the research community has produced a limited view of persons who have these illnesses and of ways to offer care.[4]

Perhaps because the symptoms of Alzheimer's disease are so frightening, there has been an insufficient effort to try to understand the inner, subjective world of persons with the diagnosis. In research articles, they are counted and the various behavioral outcomes of their cognitive declines are scored. The unique characteristics that form a whole person may become discrete variables entered into regression equations, but rarely do researchers actually converse with the person with dementia in order to try to comprehend the subjectivity of dementia.[5,6] This kind of careful listening is most often done by family members, nurses' aides, and chaplains or clergy.

In the last decade, there has been a growing awareness of possibilities for ministry with persons with dementia. Chaplains and clergy have developed remarkably creative and sensitive approaches to worship.[7,8,9] Increasing numbers of persons are receiving specialized training as chaplains with frail elderly individuals, many of whom have dementia and live in long-term care facilities. These chaplains are bringing a much-needed wholistic model of human life and experience to dementia care. They put into practice Viktor Frankl's assertion that persons must be understood as physical, psychological, social, and spiritual beings.

This paper compares Frankl's perspectives on the human search for meaning with this emergent conceptualization of dementia as presented in the work of Kitwood, Post,[10] Jones and Miesen,[11] McKim,[12] Keck[13] and others. Following a brief discussion of Frankl's[14,15,16] emphasis on human uniqueness, his wholistic view of individuals, and his description of the discovery of meaning through actions, feelings, and values, the paper turns to a more detailed analysis of the sources of meaning in the everyday lives of persons with dementia. It concludes by addressing the implications of this new view of personhood in dementia for ministry.

FRANKL'S VIEWS ON MEANING AND PERSONHOOD

Frankl often wrote about the uniqueness of human beings. People with dementia are not excluded from this description. Researchers are just beginning to address individual differences among those who suffer from dementia and they are learning that by and large, there is continuity in personality characteristics through the course of the illness, although to be sure, certain neurological changes (e.g., frontal lobe damage) produce drastic alterations in personality.[17] Other researchers are learning more about the individual differences in interpersonal relationships that are retained even in persons late in the course of the disease. These differences are most often defined in terms of styles of attachment which are established early in life.[18,19]

In Frankl's view, the quality of human uniqueness extends beyond personality differences. Each individual must find his or her own meaning in life as shaped by a "concrete personality" interacting with a "concrete situation."[20] The person with dementia retains emotional responsiveness and ways of connecting with other persons (although sometimes these forms of connection are very subtle and can only be perceived by those who "have eyes to see"). These qualities of the "concrete personality" shape the ways people experience and influence their environments.

Most people with dementia actively engage with their environments. Even when the disease progresses to the end-stages, the individual continues to interact in a unique way with the environment simply by being alive. Such a tragic condition does not remove the quality of human uniqueness that Frankl proclaimed as central to his anthropology nor does it obviate meaning. As the individual becomes more and more debilitated with a dementing illness, the responsibility for securing meaning in the interaction of a unique individual with a specific situation passes to the community–family, friends, nursing home staff. When this community is convened via common religious faith, then sacred writings and theology provide resources for understanding suffering in the light of ultimate meaning and God's enduring love.[21,22]

Reflecting the value articulated in all the world's major religions, Kitwood and others promoting a new view of dementia argue that human beings are more than their physical bodies and mental functioning. Even when the brain "can no longer tell the body what to do"[23] and when persons cannot comprehend language nor think in any way usually conceptualized as cognitive activity, still they retain personhood. This image of personhood as transcending reason, language, and thought itself stands in stark contrast to the secular, "hypercognitive"[24] bias of our postmodern culture. It is a contrast that Viktor Frankl would have seen clearly.

Kitwood has written that personhood in dementia "must be valid in terms of a psychology that focuses on experience, action, and spirituality."[25] Viktor Frankl's teaching that meaning in life is discovered in three ways resonates with Kitwood's criteria for a psychology of personhood. Frankl wrote that one achieves meaning "by creating a work or by doing a deed," "by experiencing something or encountering someone," and "by the attitude we take toward unavoidable suffering."[26] It is this latter pathway to meaning that becomes so challenging for persons with dementia and those who care for them and love them.

Suffering is unavoidable in dementia but there are many variations in the attitudes people take toward it. In Kitwood's words,

> Dementia will always have a deeply tragic aspect, both for those who are affected and for those who are close to them. There is, however, a vast difference between a tragedy, in which persons are actively involved and morally committed, and a blind and hopeless submission to fate.[27]

The horrors of the Nazi extermination camps taught Viktor Frankl that people have a choice in how they respond to suffering. They can submit helplessly and thus find no meaning in it, or they can face it defiantly and derive meaning from even the most tragic circumstances life offers.

Finding meaning in dementia does not imply romanticizing a terrible illness and the extremity of loss experienced by sufferers and their families and friends. Frankl's discovery of meaning in the camps in no way diminished the horror. Although high quality care that supports personhood can reduce many of the negative symptoms caused by malignant social environments,[28] nevertheless for most persons with dementia, there will be days filled with the agony of confusion, the frustration of not being able to communicate, and the distress of experiencing a self and a situation without recourse to thought. This is why it is so important not only to search for meaning in the lives of persons with dementia, but also to enlarge the search in order to comprehend the experience of dementia against the backdrop of ultimate meaning.

SOURCES OF MEANING IN DEMENTIA

Frankl wrote that meaning in life is variable–from person to person, and in the individual, from moment to moment. "What matters," he stated, "is not the meaning of life in general but rather the specific meaning of a person's life at a given moment."[29] Frankl did not urge people to find some kind of abstract meaning in their lives, but rather to find meaning in choices made in how to live each moment. Meaning in life only makes sense in relation to a concrete situation and life with dementia is a *very* concrete situation.

Although most people with dementia are cared for by spouses or adult children, facilities specifically designed for dementia care are increasingly being incorporated into nursing homes or are built as free-standing entities. This paper reports on an observational study conducted in a CBRF (community based residential facility) for persons with Alzheimer's disease. This facility has two connected wings, each housing up to ten residents, and is a part of a continuum of care retirement community. The design of each wing of the building incorporates many home-like features, including a living area and a kitchen/dining area where residents eat all their meals. Residents' rooms are located off short hallways connected to the main living area. Residents can freely move between the two sections of the CBRF.

For four months, the second and third authors of this paper conducted twice weekly 30 minute observations in each wing of the CBRF. They recorded all emotion displays and interpersonal interactions that occurred in public spaces. The qualitative ethnomethodology guiding this work is described by Ely.[30] It included "ongoing and intensive observing, listening, and speaking."[31] Observers sat in the public areas and recorded their observations in a notebook. When residents approached them, the observers did not hesitate to interact. In other words, they did not behave as if invisible. Once a resident noted an observer working hard at recording everything and commented, "you have the hardest job here." Every week, the three authors met to discuss the observations and they kept detailed records of these conversations. This process produced rich and detailed descriptions of the everyday life of persons who reside in a CBRF and have mid- to late-stage dementia according to the Global Deterioration Scale.[32]

The guiding philosophy of this facility promotes maximizing all remaining strengths and insuring that residents retain as much choice in their daily lives as possible. This means, for example, that they can get up in the morning on their own schedules, eat when they want, and stay in their rooms or join the group in the living area. Residents are treated as individuals, and a consistent staffing structure (two staff persons in each wing during the day) promotes continuity in their care.

Despite the profound difficulties wrought by dementia, these individuals have managed to form a community. Although some residents displayed far more overt social interaction than others, all to some degree participated in the communal life of the unit. Often, their actual conversations were distorted, but if one viewed a silent film of their interactions, one might never know that these individuals were "talking nonsense" to one another. The film would simply show several elderly friends having a normal conversation. They initiated social contact, showed sensitivity and helpfulness to one another and to staff, displayed affection for one another, argued and complained about one another's behavior. In short, they engaged in the kinds of behaviors one would expect to find among any group of adults living in community. One major difference, however, lies in the fact that they do not appear to retain grudges against one another, for their memory impairment prevents this. When one resident displayed annoyance at another's behavior, moments later, the problem appeared to be forgotten.

Another way of describing these residents' daily interactions with one another and their environment echoes the words of Viktor Frankl: they repeatedly demonstrated the defiant power of the human spirit. He wrote that "each situation in life represents a challenge" and "presents a problem . . . to solve."[33] These individuals met challenges, solved problems, and brought meaning to their lives not out of deliberate cognitive engagement with the world–a task no longer possible–but through actions, feelings, and their behavioral communication of values.

Actions

Those who do not know people with dementia might imagine that they spend their days staring blankly into the unknown. This image is often reinforced in poor quality nursing homes where the social environment is unresponsive or worse, punitive. However, in facilities that intentionally support personhood, a very different portrait of dementia emerges. Until the very end stage of the disease, most persons remain active in some way, even though their behaviors may not always be complex nor highly organized. Most measures used to assess persons with Alzheimer's disease and other dementias chart the decline of cognitive abilities and functional status. By the time they move to institutional living, they receive very low scores on evaluations of instrumental activities of daily living (IADLs) and self-care skills (ADLs). Given the bleak appearance of such evaluations, for many years researchers have paid more attention to what people with dementia *cannot* do, rather than trying to assess what they *can* do. Several recent research programs, however, have begun to remedy this problem by documenting productive behaviors[34] and everyday problem solving.[35]

Our experiences observing and interacting with these residents led us to agree with Russell who stated that it is possible to "go beyond the narrow idea of dementia as a contraction of life to a new and more complex vision of a unique and creative world of those persons living with dementia."[36] Citing the work of neurologist Oliver Sacks who so convincingly argued for the creative potential of even the most debilitating diseases, Russell posed a challenging question:

> What would happen to our understanding of the experiences of persons with dementia if we were to make some basic assumptions that there is potential in disease, even diseases as awful and frightening to us as dementia?[37]

Frankl would probably answer Russell's question by stating that by reinterpreting the behaviors of persons with dementia, we might be able to witness the retention of meaning in their lives.

At the facility where we conducted our observations, residents engaged in a number of different kinds of activities. One resident folded laundry every day while another set (and reset) the table. Residents took their dishes to the sink and wiped off the counters. They rearranged the furniture. And, of course, they wandered from one place to another in a seemingly aimless way. In addition to activities organized by staff (e.g., exercise, story-telling, simple crafts), there was a daily rhythm of small activities that, when carefully noted, revealed the way residents constructed meaning. This example was recorded by one observer (names have been changed):

> Marge gets off the couch and starts touching objects in the living room. She throws a rag on the desk, takes her plate to the sink. She stops on her way to talk to Mary. She says to a staff member, 'Are you sure you can take my plate?' She sees a knife on the counter and says, 'Shouldn't have a knife in the kitchen!' She will not give it to anyone; instead she insists on bringing it to the sink herself. 'I'm glad I caught this,' she says.

This woman was seeking to control an aspect of her environment. Just as she probably did with her own children, she was watching out for the safety of fellow residents. Although she might not be able to verbalize her concern about the knife or even recall the episode ten minutes later, still this small vignette demonstrates how she "did a deed," to paraphrase Frankl.

Feelings

The relational theory of emotions as proposed by Richard Lazarus[38] states that emotions are always about subjective connections with a situation. Too often in the past, psychologists portrayed human beings as passively responding to environmental stimuli; stereotypes about people with dementia may be a last vestige of that idea. Best known for his work on stress and coping, Lazarus has argued for many years that emotional responses result from subjective meanings constructed from interactions with the environment. This emphasis on the person/environment interaction fits well with the point of view expressed by Frankl.

In the area of feelings, one of the three pathways to meaning in Frankl's view, careful observation of people with dementia reveals a wide variety of emotions. Increasingly, researchers are learning that the emotion system in the brain is not devastated by dementing illness to the same degree as the cognitive system. Even in end-stage dementia, people can recognize facial expressions of emotions[39,40] and produce their own appropriate facial expressions.[41,42]

Our observations revealed a wide variety of emotions including anger, sadness, joy, envy, and wonder. We observed emotion contagion one day when a resident's agitation over a toileting accident spread throughout the community. Sometimes when residents expressed their feelings, their statements sounded like poetry. For example, one woman said happily, "this is the first time the sky has been all around you can see it." One day, a staff member asked a resident how she liked her dessert. She replied, "we are all quite joyful." Many times these poetic expressions elicited laughter as in the following exchange:

> Betty said to Helen, 'The sun is shining; do you think it will rain?' Helen said, 'no.' Velma joined in and said 'The stars are shining.' Betty laughed and blew air out of her mouth like it was silly.

Humor. We observed many examples of humor and laughter among residents. Most laughter in humans takes place in banal situations and not in response to an organized attempt at humor like a joke.[43] In our observations of people with dementia, we witnessed many such occasions.

Frankl stated that when humans display a sense of humor they are showing that they have mastered the "art of living."[44] To live in an institution, even a very good one such as we observed, and to suffer from an incurable, progressive, dementing illness, and still to be able to find humor in daily life, represents a triumph of the human spirit. It can even be seen as evidence of spiritual maturity, for the person whose suffering is infused with laughter reaches toward an ultimate order where suffering does not exist.[45] The person with dementia cannot articulate this, and yet these moments of good humor and laughter reveal a fundamental faith that goodness triumphs over suffering. Conrad Hyers has written that humor

> may express a certain heroic defiance in the face of life's most crushing defeats, an unquenchable nobility of spirit that refuses to permit a given fate or oppressor to have the last word–to be absolute. The human spirit has not been utterly vanquished . . . Where there is humor, there is still hope.[46]

Often, we observed that some residents seemed to be aware of their own and others' problematic cognitive functioning. For example, one day Helen observed Diane talking but not making sense. She said, "Do you understand a word she says? I don't. She's gone with the wind." Another time, Kate was upset with Velma for trying to take dishes into the bedroom area. When Helen asked what happened, Kate told her, shook her head, and laughed. On a different day, Kate was receiving a plate from Helen over Betty's head and Betty told her not to drop it on her head. Kate pretended to lose her grip and the three of them had a good laugh.

Sometimes the good natured sharing of laughter reminded the observers of children's play. For example, one time Marge picked a metal object off the floor and said "sorry" to it. She offered it to Joe, stating, "Here, you hold him for a little while." They both giggled and talked to each other about it, albeit in a way only they could understand.

As another example of how humor evoked laughter in the course of ordinary interactions, several residents began talking about the fact that it was Groundhog Day. At one point, Betty interjected, "What does the groundhog look like? He must be a popular guy!" and three elderly women all broke up in laughter.

Helen is a resident who shows considerable concern over the well-being of other residents. Perhaps some would call her "nosey" but her good nature and frequent laughter engender good will among residents. One day, the following interaction occurred between Helen and Eileen:

Helen: "Are you going out, ma?"

Eileen: "I'm going to take 5."

Helen: "You're going to take 5."

Eileen: "Wait until I get close. I can't hear you."

Helen (louder): "You're going to take 5."

Eileen: "I hope it doesn't take any longer."

Both laughed at this, to which Helen responded, "no more than 5 minutes" and touched Eileen's cheek with her finger. They laughed again.

Does this interaction make sense? Does it have meaning? Perhaps to some it sounds like mere gibberish between two senile old ladies.

And yet they *are* having a conversation; they are talking to one another and are sensitive to one another's difficulties. The tone is pleasant and they are clearly enjoying this form of human interaction. They are making meaning together. How much does it matter that neither one will remember this conversation five minutes after it ends? They are showing that they have indeed mastered the "art of living."

Values

Viktor Frankl wrote that of the three avenues to meaning in life, the most important is the attitudinal one whereby an individual embraces life-affirming values even in the face of the darkest tragic circumstances. Repeatedly, Frankl spoke of the freedom of choice given to humans that permits them to transform their suffering. This is not a call for denial of the "tragic triad" of pain, guilt, and death, but rather an affirmation of the power of the human spirit to construct meaning through the attitudes taken toward suffering. This meaning comes not from abstract philosophizing but from the kind of response one makes to the challenges life places on one's pathway through time. Life, said Frankl, expects something from people and it is up to them to respond responsibly. A person "can only answer to life by answering *for his* life."[47]

How, we might ask, can the person with dementia do this? How can life expect anything of Helen, Eileen, Joe and the others we observed? Are they not already burdened enough without having demands placed upon them to demonstrate life-affirming values?

These questions exemplify one of the last obstacles to supporting personhood and acknowledging meaning in the life of an individual with dementia. The kindly approach to these persons suffering such profound cognitive damage would seem to be to make no such demands upon them, but only to provide high quality comfort and care. And yet if we adopt this position, do we not deny their personhood and meaning in life? The prophet Micah asked "what does the Lord require of you but to do justice, and to love kindness, and to walk humbly with your God?" (Micah 6:8). The prophet did not add "but of course if you suffer from dementia you're free to disobey."

In a recently published paper, Brod and her colleagues found that some people with dementia "expressed the desire to be of more service to their community and family, and expressed pain at not having an opportunity to contribute something of worth to others and in feeling themselves to be a burden to others."[48] This conclusion resulted from administration of a newly developed instrument specifically designed to measure quality of life in persons with Alzheimer's disease. In a departure from much research on quality of life in this population, this instrument directly assesses those with Alzheimer's and does not use proxy responses from caregivers. Five scales are included: self-esteem; positive affect/humor; negative affect; feelings of belonging; and a sense of aesthetics. In answer to the self-esteem questions, people with Alzheimer's expressed their feelings about being of service to others. They seemed to be expressing the desire to be acknowledged as fully human in being able to give as well as to receive care.

In considering the ways that people with Alzheimer's might be of service to others, we are reminded of the many stories told by Frankl about his experiences in the Nazi concentration camps. Here were people living in the most degrading circumstances and yet Frankl described small acts of kindness that affirmed values and meaning in the face of suffering. A prisoner furtively passes a crust of bread to someone more hungry than himself; a nonverbal resident with dementia reaches out and pats the hand of a fellow resident who is crying. Virtue need not be writ large; it can be as simple as picking up a dropped tissue for a fellow sufferer of dementia.

The cognitive damage resulting from neurological degradation is usually understood to rob a person of intelligence. However, the view of intelligence as comprised only of cognitive abilities has been challenged in recent years, most notably by Howard Gardner who has proposed a theory of multiple intelligences.[49] Recently, Robert Emmons, a psychologist of religion and personality, has proposed the idea of "spiritual intelligence" which contains components that people with Alzheimer's and other dementias may retain, even in their most debilitated states. According to Emmons,[50] the core components of spiritual intelligence are:

1. the capacity to transcend the physical and material
2. the ability to experience heightened states of consciousness
3. the ability to sanctify everyday experience
4. the ability to utilize spiritual resources to solve problems
5. the capacity to be virtuous

Clearly, we are a long way from understanding the first four components in the lifeworlds of those with dementia. However, the fifth component–virtue–is directly observable in behavior. Emmons states that people with the capacity to engage in virtuous behaviors are able "to show forgiveness, to express gratitude, to be humble, to display compassion and wisdom."[51] Emmons does not claim that this list is exhaustive but that it represents a starting place for discussion of the "sources of human strength which enable people to function effectively in the world."[52] To use Frankl's language, they are the kinds of behaviors people engage in when they have made a choice to affirm that meaning is not obliterated by suffering.

We observed many examples of these virtues in the time we spent with residents. Nearly all responded with gratitude when a staff member helped them to do something. They also helped each other in a variety of ways. For example, some notes from observers' logs included the following:

> Al points out some lint on Mary's short. He offers her a cup to put it in. Kate seems to have taken Noreen under her wing. She gets her salt for her and takes her dishes to the table.

They also showed concern and compassion for one another. One of the most dramatic instances of this occurred one day when there was a commotion created when a resident began screaming in the bathroom. An observer recorded this interaction among residents:

> Martha continued to shout from the bathroom as a staff member tried to assist her. Mary walked up to Esther and stood there with her hands on her shoulders. As Martha let out another scream, Mary put her hands over Esther's ears. Mary then walked over to Jean and said, 'I need to talk to you.' They exchanged a few sentences that made no sense to me. Jean then said, 'I am so mixed up lately, I don't know what I'm doing.' Mary said, 'I know, I know.'

The observer noted that even though neither Jean nor Mary "made sense" to her, they seemed to understand one another. They were trying to establish social contact as a situation unfolded that provoked distress in both of them. They sought to comfort one another and to behave compassionately. Though their thoughts are scattered, their memories are gone, and their language is distorted, still something remains of their essential goodness that enables them to show virtue as best they are able.

A final example reveals a resident showing concern for the feelings of one of the observers. Mandy has very short hair and for the first few weeks, every time she conducted her observations, Betty asked her if she is a man. Mandy patiently replied that she is "a girl" but sure enough, at the next visit, Betty asked the same question. Finally, one day Mandy gently said that it hurt her feelings always to be called a man. Although Betty may not have recalled this exchange cognitively, somehow an emotional residue of empathy remained so that the following occurred at Mandy's next visit:

Betty: "You're a very pretty girl, even with the short hair."

Mandy: "Thank you, that makes me feel good. It's better than being called a man."

This exchange is then repeated verbatim by both participants.

Betty: "I like to make people feel good."

IMPLICATIONS FOR MINISTRY

In an article on aging and meaning, Melvin Kimble[53] urged scholars to employ hermeneutical phenomenology as an alternative to the scientific approach to aging and old age. In this paper, we have begun that task by examining the everyday lifeworlds of people with dementia in order to find expressions of meaning in their actions, feelings, and values. Many of the examples we have cited here occurred in less than a minute's duration and yet cumulatively, these tiny examples reveal meaning and personhood. Kimble wrote that by using the approach of hermeneutical phenomenology, we invite the old be our teachers about aging and meaning.

Do the demented old have anything to teach us? Cognitively, very little of the past remains for them. Frankl always stressed the importance of the storage of the past in memory, stating that "nothing can be undone, and nothing can be done away with."[54] But, in these people, an insidious degenerative disease has "done away with" their memories and they have lost access to the "full granaries of the past."[55] Although they have "lost their minds," people with Alzheimer's disease and other dementias have not lost their hearts. If given caring, supportive environments, where all aspects of their personhood are maintained and celebrated, then in countless ways, they demonstrate a kind of "tragic optimism,"[56] refusing to allow suffering to prevent them from "doing deeds," "experiencing," and valuing one another in spite of their suffering. In other words, they do have something to teach us about aging and meaning.

We do not wish to candy-coat dementia. Caregivers know only too well the wretched nights of wandering, the screams of fear and despair, the endless repetition of pleas for help, the incontinence, refusal to eat, and all the other disordered behaviors that can make life with a demented elder so very difficult. On the other hand, we affirm the many human strengths that are retained in persons living in a supportive environment. When these individuals are seen as whole, and not as diseased intellects, then these human strengths become more visible.

Religious affirmations of the meaning and value of human life transcend secular criteria of intelligence and productivity and offer a corrective to popular views of persons with dementia. Chaplains and clergy often clearly understand the sources of meaning in dementia. Through ritual and pastoral care, they help to organize meaningful religious actions like taking communion and therefore help to evoke religious feelings in music and prayer.

What has been typically missing in pastoral care with these individuals has been the recognition that they, too, can be held accountable for loving God and fellow human beings as well as for the kinds of attitudes they bring to suffering. This is far more challenging than designing appropriate worship experiences. However, we believe that given the emerging competent core group of persons specifically trained for ministry with people with dementia, this next step can now be taken. Affirmation of the possibilities of these expectations even for demented elders can be found in the writings of Rabbi Dayle Friedman who shows how even the most frail person in the Jewish community retains an obligation to serve God.[57]

Much work remains to be done. A chaplain at a large continuum of care community recently reported meeting a local parish clergyperson in the elevator of the facility. Making small talk, the chaplain asked him who he had come to visit and how the visits went. "Well, I have three members here," the pastor replied, "but two are out of it so I just said hello and left my card." Undoubtedly, this pastor will dutifully report to his church council that he made three pastoral calls.

Besides demanding that clergy and parish visitors become sensitive to personhood and meaning in the lives of even the most demented persons, religious communities also have a role to play in helping to change social attitudes about dementing illnesses. The work of Kitwood and others clearly articulates the difference between the "old culture" of dementia care and the emerging "new culture" that respects the actions, feelings, and spirituality of people with dementia. Religious leaders need to articulate their support for the "new culture" to policy makers, nursing home administrators, and others with the power to bring change. In other words, ministry that serves people with dementia can take many forms.

Viktor Frankl never wrote about Alzheimer's disease, but in *The Doctor and the Soul*, he mentioned how mentally retarded children are loved by their parents. He stated that "a person surrounded by loving relatives, a person who is the irreplaceable object of their love, is a person whose life has meaning, though that meaning may be only passive."[58] Sadly, some persons with dementia are not surrounded by loving relatives, although facilities like the one described here make many efforts to encourage these kinds of interactions. Sometimes, members of religious congregations can function as surrogates who affirm meaning in these persons' lives. In addition, with a new vision of meaning and personhood in dementia, family members, staff, congregational visitors, and clergy can learn profound lessons about courage in the face of suffering from these elders whose actions, feelings, and values reveal their continuing humanity.

NOTES

1. T. Kitwood, *Dementia Reconsidered: The Person Comes First* (Philadelphia: Open University Press, 1997).

2. T. Kitwood and S. Benson, *The New Culture of Dementia Care* (London: Hawker Publications, 1995).

3. Alzheimer's Association, "Statistics/prevalence." Available: http://www.alz.org/facts/rtstats.htm [1999, June 24].

4. K. A. Lyman, "Bringing the Social Back in: A Critique of the Biomedicalization of Dementia," *The Gerontologist* 29 (1989), 597-605.

5. M. Brod, A. L. Stewart, L. Sands, and P. Walton, "Conceptualization and Measurement of Quality of Life in Dementia: The Dementia Quality of Life Instrument (DQoL)." *The Gerontologist* 39 (1999), 25-35.

6. V. Cotrell, and R. Schulz, "The Perspective of the Patient with Alzheimer's Disease: A Neglected Dimension of Dementia Research." *The Gerontologist* 33 (1993), 205-211.

7. J. W. Ellor, J. Stettner, and H. Spath, "Ministry with the Confused Elderly." *Journal of Religion & Aging* 4:2 (1987), 21-33.

8. M. Richards, "Meeting the Spiritual Needs of the Cognitively Impaired," *Generations* 14:4 (1990), 63-64.

9. M. Richards and S. Seicol, "The Challenge of Maintaining Spiritual Connectedness for Persons Institutionalized with Dementia," *Journal of Religious Gerontology* 7:3 (1991), 27-40.

10. S. G. Post, *The Moral Challenge of Alzheimer's Disease* (Baltimore: Johns Hopkins Press, 1995).

11. G. M. M. Jones and B. M. L. Miesen, *Caregiving in Dementia* (London: Routledge, 1992).

12. D. K. McKim, *God Never Forgets: Faith, Hope, and Alzheimer's Disease* (Louisville, KY: Westminster John Knox Press, 1997).

13. D. Keck, *Forgetting Whose We Are: Alzheimer's Disease and the Love of God* (Nashville: Abingdon, 1996).

14. V. E. Frankl, *The Doctor and the Soul: From Psychotherapy to Logotherapy*, 2nd ed. (New York: A. A. Knopf, 1967).

15. V. E. Frankl, *The Unconscious God: Psychotherapy and Theology* (New York: Simon and Schuster, 1975).

16. V. E. Frankl, *Man's Search for Meaning* (New York: Washington Square Press, 1984).

17. S. Buckland, "Well-being, Personality and Residential Care," in *The New Culture of Dementia Care*, ed. by T. Kitwood and S. Benson (London: Hawker Publications, 1995).

18. C. Magai and C. I. Cohen, "Attachment Style and Emotion Regulation in Dementia Patients and Their Relation to Caregiver Burden," *Journal of Gerontology: Social Sciences* 53B (1998), P147-P154.

19. B. Miesen, "Attachment Theory and Dementia," in *Care Giving in Dementia*, ed. by G. Jones and B. Miesen (London: Tavistock/Routledge, 1992).

20. Frankl, 1967, 49.

21. D. D. Hopkins, "Failing Brain, Faithful Community," in *God Never Forgets: Faith, Hope, and Alzheimer's Disease*, ed. by D. K. McKim (Louisville, KY: Westminster John Knox Press, 1997).

22. S. Sapp, "Hope: The Community Looks Forward," in *God Never Forgets: Faith, Hope, and Alzheimer's Disease*, ed. by D. K. McKim (Louisville, KY: Westminster John Knox Press, 1997).

23. B. Reisberg, S. H. Ferris, M. J. DeLeon, and T. Crook, "The Global Deterioration Scale for Assessment of Primary Degenerative Dementia," *American Journal of Psychiatry* 139 (1982), 1138.

24. Post, 3.

25. Kitwood, 55.

26. Frankl, 1984, 133.

27. Kitwood, 69.

28. Ibid.

29. Frankl, 1984, 131.

30. M. Ely, *Doing Qualitative Research: Circles Within Circles* (London: The Falmer Press, 1991).

31. Ibid., 42.

32. Reisberg et al.

33. Frankl, 1984, 131.

34. C. Baum, D. F. Edwards, and N. Morrow-Howell, "Identification and Measurement of Productive Behaviors in Senile Dementia of the Alzheimer Type." *The Gerontologist* 33 (1993), 403-408.

35. S. L. Willis, R. Allen-Burge, M. M. Dolan, R. M. Bertrand, J. Yesavage, and J. J. Taylor. "Everyday Problem Solving Among Individuals with Alzheimer's Disease," *The Gerontologist* 38 (1998), 569-577.

36. C. K. Russell, "Passion and Heretics: Meaning in Life and Quality of Life of Persons with Dementia," *Journal of the American Geriatrics Society* 44 (1996), 1401.

37. Ibid.

38. R. S. Lazarus, *Emotion and Adaptation* (New York: Oxford University Press, 1991).

39. M. S. Albert, C. Cohen, and E. Koff, "Perception of Affect in Patients with Dementia of the Alzheimer Type." *Archives of Neurology* 48 (1991), 791-795.

40. T. Zandi, M. Cooper, and L. Garrison, "Facial Recognition: A Cognitive Study of Elderly Dementia Patients and Normal Older Adults," *International Psychogeriatrics* 4 (1992), 215-221.

41. K. Asplund, A. Norberg, R. Adolfsson, and H. M. Waxman, "Facial Expressions in Severely Demented Patients–A Stimulus-Response Study of Four Patients with Dementia of the Alzheimer Type." *International Journal of Geriatric Psychiatry* 6 (1991), 599-606.

42. C. Magai, C. Cohen, D. Gomberg, C. Malatesta, and C. Culver, "Emotional Expression during Mid- to Late-stage Dementia," *International Psychogeriatrics* 8 (1996), 383-395.

43. R. R. Provine, "Laughter," *American Scientist* 84 (1996), 38-45.

44. Frankl, 1984, 64.

45. S. H. McFadden, "Authentic Humor as an Expression of Spiritual Maturity," in *Spiritual Maturity in the Later Years*, ed. by J. J. Seeber (New York: Haworth, 1990).

46. C. Hyers, *The Comic Vision and the Christian Faith* (New York: Pilgrim Press, 1981), 36.

47. Frankl, 1967, xiii.

48. Brod et al., 33.

49. H. Gardner, *Frames of Mind: The Theory of Multiple Intelligences* (New York: Basic, 1983).

50. R. A. Emmons, *The Psychology of Ultimate Concerns*: *Motivation and Spirituality in Personality* (New York: Guilford, 1999), 164.

51. Ibid., 166.

52. Ibid., 167.

53. M. A. Kimble, "Aging and the Search for Meaning," in *Spiritual Maturity in the Later Years*, ed. by J. J. Seeber (New York: Haworth, 1990).

54. Frankl, 1984, 144.

55. Ibid., 143-144.

56. Ibid., 162.

57. D. Friedman, "Spiritual Challenges of Nursing Home Life," in *Aging, Spirituality, and Religion: A Handbook*, ed. by M. A. Kimble, S. H. McFadden, J. W. Ellor, and J. J. Seeber (Minneapolis: Fortress, 1995).

58. Frankl, 1967, 39.

Bridging Psychology and Theology
When Counseling Older Adults

James W. Ellor, PhD

SUMMARY. Seniors raise many questions for counselors; some of these questions directly impact what can be called spiritual concerns. Yet, finding a consistent definition of what a "spiritual concern" is has challenged all of the major counseling professions. In this paper the author calls upon the work of Paul Tillich in dialogue with that of Viktor Frankl to bridge the theological definitions of spiritual concern with psychological intervention. *[Article copies available for a fee from The Haworth Document Delivery Service: 1-800-342-9678. E-mail address: <getinfo@haworthpressinc.com> Website: <http://www.HaworthPress.com>]*

This paper presents the case of Mrs. Maggie McFarlane, who struggles with issues of body image that reflect feelings influenced, in part, by her now deceased father and husband. This case is followed throughout the paper as an example of the need for a spiritual assessment tool that points to a treatment strategy for older parishioners. The basis for this assessment tool and strategy is found by employing a theory of explanation found in the work of the theologian, Paul Tillich and the psychiatrist, Viktor Frankl. Tillich understands the human ideal as dwelling in a balance between polarities. Spiritual balance offers the ideal which is then measured against the current issues and con-

---

James W. Ellor, PhD, is Associate Director, Center for Aging, Religion and Spirituality and Professor of the Department of Human Services National-Louis University.

[Haworth co-indexing entry note]: "Bridging Psychology and Theology When Counseling Older Adults." Ellor, James W. Co-published simultaneously in *Journal of Religious Gerontology* (The Haworth Pastoral Press, an imprint of The Haworth Press, Inc.) Vol. 11, No. 3/4, 2000, pp. 87-102; and: *Viktor Frankl's Contribution to Spirituality and Aging* (ed: Melvin A. Kimble) The Haworth Pastoral Press, an imprint of The Haworth Press, Inc., 2000, pp. 87-102. Single or multiple copies of this article are available for a fee from The Haworth Document Delivery Service [1-800-342-9678, 9:00 a.m. - 5:00 p.m. (EST). E-mail address: getinfo@haworthpressinc.com].

87

cerns of the parishioner, in this case Mrs. Maggie McFarlane. The work of Viktor Frankl then offers the tools to work with the senior to gather resources to address problems and celebrate strengths. The work of Frankl and Tillich comes together at their root as both are built upon the existential work of Martin Heidegger. Both theorists understand essence to precede existence which breaks open counseling paradigms for a spiritual presence that is challenged by approaches that must begin with existence and learn life without benefit of the spirit. By identifying spiritual balance and placing it in the context of the existential struggles and search for meaning, the therapist has an approach to the client which both identifies spiritual concern and offers intervention that can be employed in concert with the allied disciplines found in community and long term care facilities.

Mrs. Maggie McFarlane is a woman of the world. Born in Scotland, her family emigrated to the United States when she was a teenager. Mrs. McFarlane married her husband Jake when he returned from the War. Jake and Maggie were happily married for forty-two years until Jake had a heart attack and died. Jake had been in the shipping business and often traveled the world with Maggie. Maggie is fond of saying that she liked Jake because he was so much like her father. Both men seemed to surround themselves with good-looking people. Both wore only the nicest clothes. "Appearances" in many ways were very important to both of them. Maggie and Jake have two daughters, who were also brought up to pay attention to "appearance."

The McFarlane family attends their local Presbyterian Church on a regular basis. Both Maggie and Jake were raised in the church and are particularly fond of the intellectual stimulation that they experience from worship. Maggie has been a member of the board of deacons and the board of elders; Jake had been an elder.

Recently Maggie was diagnosed with colon cancer. Maggie said, "it all happened so fast." She was diagnosed and in surgery in a matter of days. She insisted that no one discussed the possibility of a colostomy with her, prior to surgery. After surgery, Maggie refused all visitors, even family, as she did not want anyone to see her. One of the nurses reported to Maggie's daughter that she was refusing to learn how to care for her colostomy, insisting that the nurses do everything. Her seclusion continued at home. Maggie insisted that the Home Health nurse do all of the stoma maintenance. This meant that she had to hire a full time nursing staff to meet her needs 24 hours a day. Her daughters became progressively alarmed. They understood that she was capable of taking care of the colostomy herself and did not really need the nurses. Possibly more importantly, this usually gregarious person was shutting everyone out. Nothing that they said to her seemed to have any impact. When Maggie's daughters tried to talk with her about her colostomy, she diverted the discussion, by asking the question, "Why does not God let me die?"

After much frustration, one of her daughters turned to her church. Pastor John began by working with the daughter to begin to understand the situation. He then worked with her to gain her mother's permission for him to visit. On their first visit, John listened to Maggie's discussion of her surgery. He noted that there was no mention of the colostomy. As he listened, he also noted that she seemed to be searching for his acceptance, yet she was not clear as to what she wanted him to accept. She also verbalized a great deal of anger with God, for allowing this to happen.

Based on his work with her daughter and his own clinical experience, John gently queried about her need for acceptance. Slowly this turned to a discussion about her perception as to how her husband and father would feel about her surgery. With this, she immediately terminated the session and asked him to leave.

After a few days, Mrs. McFarlane called John and asked him to come to see her again. When he arrived, she apologized for her behavior and began to talk about her husband and father's obsession with appearance. As she talked, she visibly seemed to lift a burden. While John did not say much in this session, after he left he was told that she began to talk with her friends and to take over her own colostomy care, and even came to church the next Sunday. John was then able to refer her to one of the Befrienders in the church for additional support.

Cases like that of Maggie challenge therapists to hear more than the obvious adjustment issues. While some would treat her for depression, others see a person who is verbalizing spiritual and religious issues and seek a broader range of skills to support her in the counseling experience. For the therapist to pick up on the spiritual or religious aspects of this case, a basis for this type of intervention needs to be appended to his or her paradigm. Traditional paradigms in counseling have no room for religious or spiritual intervention, as they are unable to affirm anything more than the human condition. Theorists from some paradigms, Freud, Ellis, and others, were distinctly hostile toward religious and spiritual concerns. Others seem to be silent. This often leaves therapists who are personally concerned about spiritual concerns without a solid paradigmal basis for intervention. Thus, often the spiritual and religious concern is ignored, or it is addressed from the personal faith position of the therapist.

Pastoral counselors and other persons concerned with spiritual matters have recently begun to examine the nature and role of the religious and spiritual concerns in counseling. The simplest approach to integrating spiritual and/or religious issues raised in counseling by the senior is to treat it like any other belief or behavior. Whether discussing the Lions Club or a church, relationships and beliefs are expressed that reflect these groups that are addressed every day in counseling. This approach does not necessarily challenge the counselor to move outside of his or her normal pattern of listening and intervention.

The movement to interpreting these concerns beyond their surface value as behaviors or beliefs causes the therapist to reexamine his or her "theory of explanation" or paradigm. Secular Humanism, which offers the most common theory of explanation for counselors, is by definition inadequate to fully explore the spiritual questions due to the central focus on the human. If reality focuses only on the human, there is no basis to discuss the spiritual in relationship to anything that is larger than that which can be perceived by the human experience. To address this weakness, bridges are needed to be developed between theology and psychology that will afford a more complete dialogue toward viable explanations of human behavior.

The work of Viktor Frankl offers important first steps toward developing the necessary bridges between theology and psychology. Frankl's work is based, in part, on the philosophical work of Martin Heidegger. Often categorized with other existential thinkers, Frankl offers the potential to address more than the behaviors of religion through his understanding of the Noetic or spiritual aspect of the person. Frankl's anthropology offers the possibility that the person is more than what is born and dies. Rather, Frankl understands that there is something of the human spirit that precedes the conception of the person. In placing the possibility of essence coming before existence, Frankl acknowledges the spiritual aspect of the person as more than the free will and choices of the individual and/or his or her environment. Carl Jung is the only other traditional theorist who makes this accommodation through his understanding of the collective unconscious.

The work of Viktor Frankl or Logotherapy offers a therapeutic basis for the inclusion of the spiritual within a counseling practice. However, Frankl is very clear that he is addressing the human spirit. To fully understand the spiritual nature of the person the work of Paul Tillich will also be briefly explored. Tillich also based his systematic theology on the work of Martin Heidegger. This commonality offers consistent opportunity for dialogue between the work of the psychologist, Viktor Frankl and the theologian, Paul Tillich. The net result is a much fuller understanding of the nature of the spiritual and the ramifications of the human condition.

FRANKL AND THE SPIRITUAL

"A well-known psychiatrist once remarked that Western humanity has turned from the priest to the doctor."[1] This transition from religion to medicine was promoted by early psychiatry, especially Sigmund Freud. However, it reflects a struggle in the work of Viktor Frankl. Possibly one of the most misunderstood aspects of his work, the definition and role of the spiritual, is key to his theory of explanation. On the one hand, Frankl is clear that Logotherapy "is not intended to serve as a substitute for religion."[2] Frankl consistently discusses the centrality of the spiritual aspect of the person to human existence. To understand this seeming contradiction, the reader must first understand the word "spirit" in the German Language.

Dr. Frankl suggests that any European, when confronted with the word *spirit*, would need to understand which type of spirit is being discussed. Dr. Frankl notes that in German the root word *geist* (spirit) has several forms; the principle distinction for our purposes is between *geistig* which is the intellectual, mental, non-religious spirit (the ability for the individual to transcend beyond themselves) and *geistlich* which is the sacred or religious definition (the relationship with God).[3] The theologian Paul Tillich makes this distinction in his writing by talking about spirit with a small "s" and Spirit with a capital "S." Unfortunately, Frankl makes no such distinction. Bulka notes that "the translators of Frankl's works used the term spirituality loosely, thus distorting the precise meaning as it is evident from the German. Frankl, in his own English writings, carefully avoids this misuse by using the terms 'noological' and 'noetic,' to differentiate from the psychological and psychic, respectively, and to distinguish from the spiritual dimension in its religious sense."[4] For Frankl, the spiritual aspect of the person is the noological dimension. Frankl notes, "the noological dimension may rightly be defined as the dimension of uniquely human phenomena."[5] It is within this dimension that Frankl understands "man's search for meaning."[6]

While Logotherapy focuses on the distinctly human aspects of life, clearly it borders on the religious. Frankl views religion as a human phenomenon which must be viewed positively by the therapist. However, he is clear that psychotherapy is not religion. The distinction between geistig and geistlich offers a critical point of departure. Both uses of the root word geist (spirit) have in common an understanding of transcendence. Transcendence at the human level reflects the capacity to care about others more than one necessarily cares about oneself. Frankl puts it this way, "What here comes in is no more nor less than the self-transcendent quality of human existence. The question, What am I if I do it for my own sake only–requires the answer–In no event a truly human being. For it is characteristic constituent of human existence that it transcends itself, that it reaches out for something other than itself."[7] It is this ability to transcend that constitutes the Noetic aspect of the person. Frankl writes, "man transcends his environment toward the world; but more than this, he also transcends his being toward an ought. When he does this, he rises above the level of the somatic and the psychic and enters the realm of the genuinely human. This real is constituted by a new dimension, the noetic, the dimension of the spirit."[8] In this way, the human spirit, geistig, reflects many of the values for human interaction that are found in religion. Frankl notes, "truly, self-transcendence is the essence of human existence."[9] Meaning is not an intra-psychic philosophical concept. Rather, it is a critical aspect of spirituality that points to humanity's fullest capacity for "being."

Frankl understands "the striving to find a meaning in one's life as the primary motivational force in man."[10] Three key concepts[11] elucidate the key role of meaning, "freedom of the will," "the will to meaning," and "the meaning of life." Frankl acknowledges that the body can be placed in bondage, but key to the therapeutic value of Logotherapy is the understanding that each person has a freedom of will. In other words, while one's body can be held in chains, no one can take away the individual's right to choose his or her attitude toward the situation or persons. We have a freedom to choose value orientations, a freedom to choose transcendence over the primacy of the self. This freedom resides, however, in the context of responsibility, responsibility toward oneself and others.

Frankl says that the motivation to choose the transcendent values comes from the will to meaning. The Will to Meaning "may be seen as the mediating principle between the human being, the 'subject,' and the world of values, the 'object.'"[12] Human beings are free to choose and have the capacity to will toward meaning. Frankl is clear that we are not pushed toward meaning. Rather the will to meaning is a spiritual act. Frankl frequently contrasts the will to meaning with the pleasure principle of Sigmund Freud or the will to power principle of Alfred Adler which suggests that the primary motivation of humanity is to strive toward pleasure or power respectively. The drive to pleasure or the will to power according to Frankl is self-defeating. The more the individual pursues each, the more one is alienated from others. This type of isolation leads to greater anxiety and not the fulfillment of our "being." Frankl puts it this way, "My own reaction to this theorizing is that I would not be willing to live for the sake of my 'defense mechanisms,' much less to die for the sake of my 'reaction formations.'"[13]

In Logotherapy the third pillar is that there is always a meaning of life. There is an unconditional meaningfulness that is always available for us to grasp. Illustrated by Frankl's many examples, meaning is there to be found. However, no one can give meaning to someone else. Meaning is realized through values that are available if the individual chooses to grasp or see them. "Meaning is what is meant by a person who asks me a question, or by a situation which, too, implies a question and calls for an answer."[14] It is the product of a triad of *creative, experiential,* and *attitudinal* values. These attitudinal values are further defined by reflection on the individual's values toward pain, guilt, and death.[15]

The impact of this concept of the spiritual suggests that "rather than being concerned with any inner condition, be it pleasure or homeostasis, man is oriented toward the world out there, and within this world, he is interested in meanings to fulfill, and in other human beings."[16] Suffering can then be challenged by the freedom of the will to determine how one will view the situation. Meaning can be found, even in tragedy. It is this human capacity to will to meaning that truly sets humanity aside from other life forms.

While the spiritual or Noetic nature of humanity reflects the transcendent nature of human existence, Frankl understands that there is a human capacity to will to understand God. Meaning at the human level is down to earth. However, Frankl also understands that there is "some sort of meaning that is 'up in heaven,' as it were; some sort of ultimate meaning."[17] He notes that "the more comprehensive the meaning, the less comprehensible it is."[18] This ultimate meaning eludes scientific definition, but can be found in religion. Frankl defines religion as man's search for *ultimate meaning.*[19] He goes on to explain that religion guides the individual to find the ultimate meaning of life. If this is true, then he notes that belief and faith are another way of saying trust in an ultimate meaning. Frankl notes, "once we have conceived of religion in this way–that is, in the widest possible sense–there is no doubt that psychiatrists are entitled also to investigate this phenomenon, although only its human aspect is accessible to a psychological exploration."

Frankl goes on to define God as "not one thing among others but being itself or Being."[20] This ultimate Being cannot be placed in the same understanding of reality as other beings, therefore human beings know it as a symbol of Being. Religion can then be defined as the organizational source of symbols of ultimate meaning and being itself. Therefore, Frankl notes, "to be religious is to have found the answer to the question, What is the meaning of life?"[21]

TILLICH AND THE SPIRITUAL

The work of Paul Tillich like that of Viktor Frankl offers a rich approach to understanding a "theory of explanation" that is large enough to include an understanding of the spiritual which moves beyond observing the behaviors of religious expression. Tillich like Frankl bases much of his work on that of Martin Heidegger. This existential context is reflected in his anthrocentric approach to his theological system. For Tillich, God is understood to be the "ground of being." As such, he is beyond human understanding or definition. Thus, when we speak of God, we reflect our human interpretation or the symbols of our understanding of God's nature. While God is unconditional, human beings are finite and therefore struggle with their existential existence. For both Frankl and Tillich the boundaries of this existence are the source of much of the human pain experienced by our clients.

Spiritual assessment in this context needs to be understood in light of the larger concepts put forward in Tillich's systematic theology. The temptation in the field is to try to isolate the spiritual aspect of the person in the same way that physical, social and psychological elements have been targeted. It should be understood that for Tillich, as with most theologians, the spirit cannot be isolated from the creator, sustainer and redeemer dimensions of the ground of being. In an effort to outline an approach, rather than offering a comprehensive discussion of Tillich's entire systematic, in this section, the focus will be on the spiritual. However, this discussion is based upon his entire theological structure.

The term spiritual was often not used by Tillich as he found it to be an overworked term. However, it remained central to his system. As a theologian, Tillich's systematic theology explores matters of a spiritual nature in significantly greater depth than does Frankl. Like Frankl he understands the distinction between geistig and geistlich. However, Tillich consistently makes this distinction by referring to spirit (small "s") and Spirit (capital "S"). Tillich suggests that "spirit as a dimension of life unites the power of being with the meaning of being. Spirit can be defined as the actualization of power and meaning in unity. Within the limits of our experience this happens only in man–in man as a whole and in all the dimensions of life which are present in him ... without this experience of spirit as the unity of power and meaning in himself, man would not have been able to express the revelator experience of 'God present' in the term 'Spirit' or 'Spiritual Presence.'"[22]

For Tillich, like Frankl, the spiritual nature of the person is exemplified by the actualization of meaning. Meaning for Tillich is facilitated by culture which creates many different possibilities of meaning for the individual. Like Frankl, each individual must come to his or her own understanding as to what it is. However, instead of starting from universal values, it starts from a universe of options for meaning found in culture. Meaning then, is the "actualization of what is potential in the bearer of the spirit–man."[23] Tillich notes that "without knowing what *spirit* is, one cannot know what *Spirit* is."[24] Therefore the actualization of meaning which is spirit is a first step toward knowing the Spirit who is in relationship with God.

Tillich understands that it is the ambiguous nature of human existence that brings us to seek or have a will to meaning to use Frankl's concept. In doing so, each step toward grasping our human understanding of meaning brings us closer to the symbols of the Divine Spirit. Like Frankl, the human interaction with God and humanity is understood to be a relationship. Tillich notes, "the relation between Spirit and spirit is usually answered by the metaphorical statement that the divine Spirit dwells and works in the human spirit."[25]

For Tillich and Frankl, the spirit is actualized in relationship with the human condition. Where Frankl characterizes this as reflecting the Tragic Triad of *pain, guilt and death*,[26] Tillich sees it as a part of the larger human condition. Both Tillich and Frankl would see the nature of the person in light of the wholistic dimensions of the person. Frankl understands the physical, psychological and noetic dimensions. For Tillich this is somewhat more complex. As seen in Figure 1, there are four key concepts contained in Tillich's understanding of the whole person. The first reflects the traditional elements of the whole person. These *organic* elements are the mechanical, chemical and biological elements of the person. As seen in Figure 2, each of these dimensions can be seen as a struggle between two polar dynamics. It should be noted that Tillich understands a polar relationship not as the exposition of opposites, but rather as two dynamics in creative tension with one another. The traditional basis for wholism then is understood in terms of the polar relationships between health and disease, chemical substances and the process of living organisms, and self-alteration and self-preservation. The ideal for Tillich in these polarities is "centered being." To be centered is to understand that the term "centeredness" is derived from the geometrical circle and metaphorically[27] applied to the structure of a being in which an effect exercised on one part has consequences for all other parts, directly or indirectly.[28] Thus, to be centered is to be in balance between the various dynamics of human existence. For Tillich, to rest too close to any one side of the polarity, or to be out of touch with one's polarities, is to be out of center and by implication indicative of pathology.

With the concept of the spiritual center, Tillich refines the search for meaning in terms of the balance of the polarities that are reflective of human existence. These polarities extend to the psychological dimension in the form of the polarity of change and stability. Change or the transitory nature of human existence according to Frankl is a part of life and thus aging. Stability, or what the gerontologist Robert Atchley would refer to as "continuity," is perceived to be sought, particularly in times of transition. Fully defining the human condition are three key polarities, individualization and participation, dynamics and form, and freedom and destiny. These polarities offer a basis for interpreting many of the struggles encountered within human existence. The distinctive aspects of the spirit reflect the influences of culture, morality and religion.

One can see from this brief discussion of Tillich's system that it offers a rich and dynamic model from which to understand both Frankl's logotherapy as well as a larger view of Christian faith. Many

FIGURE 1

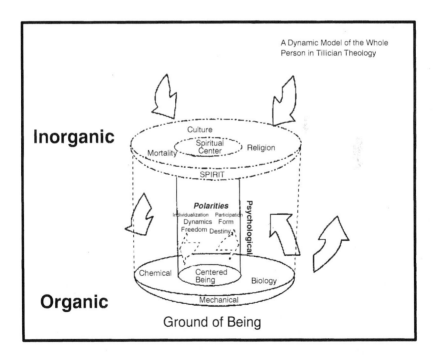

A Dynamic Model of the Whole Person in Tillician Theology

Inorganic

Culture

Spiritual Center

Mortality   Religion

SPIRIT

Polarities
Individualization Participation
Dynamics Form
Freedom Destiny

Psychological

Chemical   Centered Being   Biology

Mechanical

Organic

Ground of Being

FIGURE 2

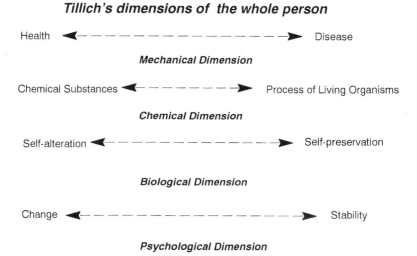

Tillich's dimensions of the whole person

Health ◀— — — — — — — — — — — — — —▶ Disease

Mechanical Dimension

Chemical Substances ◀— — — — — — —▶ Process of Living Organisms

Chemical Dimension

Self-alteration ◀— — — — — — — — — — —▶ Self-preservation

Biological Dimension

Change ◀— — — — — — — — — — — — — — —▶ Stability

Psychological Dimension

topics not discussed here can also be brought into this discussion, including the nature of faith, hope and love. Where Tillich's concepts are strong on theory, Frankl's work offers counseling application.

COMBINING THE TWO THEORIES
IN THE CASE OF MAGGIE AND JAKE

To understand Maggie's situation is to begin by understanding that the heart of her existential crisis is defined by her finite nature as a human being. Whether one starts from the frailty of her need for "appearances," in the context of having cancer or the very basic threat to her existence often symbolized by a cancer diagnosis, the initial diagnosis of an existential crisis is clear. However, to refine this in spiritual terms, the crisis is developed by her loss of center, particularly in the areas of the mechanical dimensions of health and disease and in the psychological dimensions of dynamics and form.

Tillich notes that "centeredness is a universal phenomenon."[29] All organisms encounter the need for balance with all other organisms. In the case of cancer, there is a clear lack of balance found in the nature of the disease. Tillich notes, "many diseases, especially infectious ones, can be understood as an organism's inability to return to its self-identity."[30] This lack of ability to return to self-identity tips the balance from health to disease. Most critical is the assault on the ontological polarity of dynamics and form. Tillich notes: "finitude also transforms the polarity of dynamics and form into tension which produces the threat of a possible break and anxiety about this threat. Dynamics drives toward form, in which being is actual and has the power of resisting nonbeing. But at the same time dynamics is threatened because it may lose itself in rigid forms, and if it tries to break through them, the result may be chaos, which is the loss of both dynamics and form. Human vitality tends to embody itself in cultural creations, forms, and institutions through the exercise of creative intentionality. But every embodiment endangers the vital power precisely by giving it actual being. Man is anxious about the threat of a final form in which his vitality will be lost, and he is anxious about the threat of a chaotic formlessness in which both vitality and intentionality will be lost."[31]

As we come to realize the significance of the threat to Maggie's need for a centered self, we can see that these elements of the spiritual crisis also inhibit her search for meaning. Critical in this analysis, is both Frankl and Tillich's understanding of the role of freedom of choice of attitude for recovery. Therapeutic intervention needs to remind Maggie of her need for balance or centering in the face of adversity and suffering. Maggie poses the question, "Why will God not let me die?" This all too familiar query is often answered theologically with the statement, "God must have some ongoing purpose for you." Frankl and Tillich would see this as a crisis of meaning. Frankl specifically coined the diagnosis "existential vacuum" to describe the persons like Maggie who are unable to see meaning in their life. With balance, the existential crisis can be ministered to through the search for meaning. Frankl's rules for this quest include the belief on the part of the therapist that there is always meaning out there, the therapist cannot give meaning to Maggie, and that Maggie can determine how she is to perceive this assault on her appearance. Along the way, Maggie can be reminded of the cultural role of both her definition of proper appearance and thus its impact on her former understanding of meaning in her life. A new perspective of this cultural influence may allow her to reject the former need for perfection and accept a new image that more fully experiences her finite nature.

While not fully addressed in this document, the aspect of the significance of her husband and father in Maggie's body image transition is also clearly supported by understanding the role of the historical sources of meaning and thus input on body image as represented by these key persons in her life. The nature of time according to both Tillich and Frankl suggests that Maggie cannot go back to her now deceased parent and spouse to discuss their input on her need for appearances. However, the existential understanding of the present as building on the past allows the therapist to keep her father and spouse in mind as he works with her to move beyond the ambiguity of her current crisis toward the fulfillment of her centered self.

For Maggie her father and husband had become ghosts from her past in that their agenda for appearances had in some way become her need to fulfill their expectations. These expectations haunted her as she faced the realities of her colostomy. She could not see that a colostomy need not be a debilitating condition. Rather, it can be managed and the individual lead a normal life. It is a mistake to translate Maggie's obsession with the concerns of her departed male relatives as a ghostly apparition. Rather, Frankl and Tillich would see their values and for Tillich their cultural context as threatening her balance between health and disease. By experiencing the colostomy as disease and losing the tension with her greater health, Maggie gave up her search for meaning in favor of the disease. The therapeutic intervention needs to become aware of the admonitions of these important male figures, while helping her to see them in the context of their meaning.

CONCLUSION

Pastoral counseling benefits twice from bridging theology and psychology. First, by offering insights that can be helpful to Maggie and her family. Second, by offering conceptual tools that draw together the strengths of the field. However, the term spiritual needs to be defined. By starting from the systematic theology of Paul Tillich, a rich definition can be offered. With this definition, the work of Viktor Frankl can be enhanced to understand both the human spirit as well as the "ground of being," or search for ultimate meaning. In the work of Viktor Frankl, the therapist can also find the therapeutic tools to support the client.

This system requires the therapist to learn both an extensive theology as well as a psychological approach which offers a challenge. However, like any other complicated concept, the rewards for grasping this material are also richer.

REFERENCES

1. Frankl, Viktor E. *The Doctor and the Soul*. New York: Vintage Books. 1955. xv.

2. Frankl, Viktor E. *The Doctor and the Soul*. New York: Vintage Books. 1955. xii-xiii.

3. Frankl, Viktor E. *Psychotherapy and Existentialism*. New York: Washington Square Press. 1967. 65.

4. Bulka, Reuven P. *Work, Love, Suffering, Death: A Jewish/Psychological Perspective Through Logotherapy*. Northvale: Jason Aronson, Inc. 1979. 47.

5. Frankl, Viktor E. *The Unconscious God*. New York: Washington Square Press. 1975. 13.

6. Frankl, Viktor E. *The Unconscious God*. New York: Washington Square Press. 1975. 13.

7. Bulka, Reuven P. *Work, Love, Suffering, Death: A Jewish/Psychological Perspective Through Logotherapy*. Northvale: Jason Aronson, Inc. 1979. 94.

8. Frankl, Viktor E. *Psychotherapy and Existentialism*. New York: Washington Square Press. 1967. 134.

9. Frankl, Viktor E. *Psychotherapy and Existentialism*. New York: Washington Square Press. 1967. 134.

10. Frankl, Viktor E. *Man's Search for Meaning*. New York: Washington Square Press. 1963. 154

11. Frankl refers to them as the three pillars of Logotherapy. Frankl, Viktor. *The Will to Meaning: Foundations and Applications of Logotherapy*. New York: New American Library. 1969. 16.

12. Bulka, Reuven P. *Work, Love, Suffering, Death: A Jewish/Psychological Perspective Through Logotherapy*. Northvale: Jason Aronson, Inc. 1979. 48.

13. Frankl, Viktor E. *Psychotherapy and Existentialism*. New York: Washington Square Press. 1967. 25. and Frankl, Viktor. *The Will to Meaning: Foundations and Applications of Logotherapy*. New York: New American Library. 1969. 54.

14. Frankl, Viktor. *The Will to Meaning: Foundations and Applications of Logotherapy*. New York: New American Library. 1969. 62.

15. Frankl, Viktor. *The Will to Meaning: Foundations and Applications of Logotherapy*. New York: New American Library. 1969. 73.

16. Frankl, Viktor. *The Will to Meaning: Foundations and Applications of Logotherapy*. New York: New American Library. 1969. 73.

17. Frankl, Viktor E. *Man's Search for Ultimate Meaning*. New York: Insight Books. 1997. 143.

18. Frankl, Viktor E. *Man's Search for Ultimate Meaning*. New York: Insight Books. 1997. 143.

19. Frankl, Viktor E. *The Unconscious God.* New York: Washington Square Press. 1975. 13.

20. Frankl, Viktor E. *Man's Search for Ultimate Meaning.* New York: Insight Books. 1997. 143.

21. Frankl, Viktor E. *Man's Search for Ultimate Meaning.* New York: Insight Books. 1997. 153.

22. Tillich, Paul. *Systematic Theology.* Vol. III. Chicago: University of Chicago Press. 1963. 111.

23. Tillich, Paul. *Systematic Theology.* Vol. III. Chicago: University of Chicago Press. 1963. 84.

24. Tillich, Paul. *Systematic Theology.* Vol. III. Chicago: University of Chicago Press. 1963. 22.

25. Tillich, Paul. *Systematic Theology.* Vol. III. Chicago: University of Chicago Press. 1963. 111.

26. Frankl, Viktor. *The Will to Meaning: Foundations and Applications of Logotherapy.* New York: New American Library. 1969. 73.

27. Atchley, Robert C. The Continuity of the Spiritual Self. In *Aging, Spirituality, and Religion*, edited by Melvin A. Kimble, S. H. McFadden, J. W. Ellor and J. J. Seeber. Minneapolis: Fortress Press. 1995. 68-74.

28. Tillich, Paul. *Systematic Theology.* Vol. III. Chicago: University of Chicago Press. 1963. 33.

29. Tillich, Paul. *Systematic Theology.* Vol. III. Chicago: University of Chicago Press. 1963. 34.

30. Tillich, Paul. *Systematic Theology.* Vol. III. Chicago: University of Chicago Press. 1963. 35.

31. Tillich, Paul. *Systematic Theology.* Vol. I. Chicago: University of Chicago Press. 1956. 200.

Logotherapy in the Care
of the Terminally Ill

Paul J. Brat, MD

SUMMARY. Logotherapy is very useful in dealing with a person with a terminal illness in that such a person often feels that life is meaningless. Viktor Frankl asserts that each person's life has a unique meaning even when the person is confronted with a terminal condition over which he/she seemingly has little control. It is the role of the logotherapist to help the person to discover that unique meaning within himself/ herself. The logotherapist does not provide the meaning, but rather assists the person in discovering his/her own meaning. This article explores the various ways by which meaning may be discovered through the methods of logotherapy. *[Article copies available for a fee from The Haworth Document Delivery Service: 1-800-342-9678. E-mail address: <getinfo@haworthpressinc.com> Website: <http://www.HaworthPress.com>]*

We are all terminally ill! This statement reflects the fact that we are finite creatures and live under the threat of nonbeing (Tillich, 1952, 32). For the purposes of this paper, however, I will use a narrower definition of terminal illness. The hospice movement in the United States defines terminal illness as incurable illness where life expectancy is measured in weeks or months rather than years (Rossman, 1977, 155). Medicare limits eligibility for hospice benefits to those who have a life expectancy of less than six months. Also, for purposes of this paper, I will be discussing terminal illness in terms of incurable cancer since this is overwhelmingly the most common terminal condition seen in a hospice setting.

[Haworth co-indexing entry note]: "Logotherapy in the Care of the Terminally Ill." Brat, Paul J. Co-published simultaneously in *Journal of Religious Gerontology* (The Haworth Pastoral Press, an imprint of The Haworth Press, Inc.) Vol. 11, No. 3/4, 2000, pp. 103-117; and: *Viktor Frankl's Contribution to Spirituality and Aging* (ed: Melvin A. Kimble) The Haworth Pastoral Press, an imprint of The Haworth Press, Inc., 2000, pp. 103-117. Single or multiple copies of this article are available for a fee from The Haworth Document Delivery Service [1-800-342-9678, 9:00 a.m. - 5:00 p.m. (EST). E-mail address: getinfo@haworthpressinc.com].

103

Logotherapy is a system of therapy introduced by Viktor Frankl, a Viennese psychiatrist. Logotherapy is based on three concepts: (1) the freedom of will (2) the will to meaning and (3) the meaning of life (Frankl, 1969, vii).

By freedom of will, Frankl does not mean to imply that persons are free from conditions, be they biological, psychological or sociological in nature. For finite beings, freedom is always freedom within limits. Cancer, for example, is a condition over which a person has little control once it becomes inoperable and incurable. However, a person "is, and always remains, free to take a stand toward these conditions; he always retains the freedom to choose his attitude toward them" (Frankl, 1967, 3).

The will to meaning is used by Frankl to state that each person is seeking a meaning which is unique and specific to one's own life. "Man's search for meaning is the primary motivation in his life" (Frankl, 1959, 105). This means that each person must try to find the true meaning of the question which life asks of them. These questions must be answered responsibly. "Man is responsible for giving the *right* answer to a question, for finding the *true* meaning of a situation" (Frankl, 1969, 62). The person with incurable cancer often asks the question–'Why did this happen to me?' This is the wrong question. The right question is–"Given the fact that I have an incurable cancer, how am I to respond to this situation?"

The third concept in logotherapy, the meaning of life, implies that each person's life does in fact have a meaning. This fact is often denied by persons, especially by those with a terminal condition. To them, life seems meaningless since they are confronted not only with the transitoriness of life, but are also often plagued by what Frankl describes as the tragic triad of human existence: pain, death and guilt (Frankl, 1969, ix). It is in this situation that logotherapy is particularly helpful. Logotherapy focuses on the future, on the meanings yet to be fulfilled by the patient even when they feel as though life has no further meaning (Frankl, 1959, 104). The logotherapist cannot show the patient what the meaning is, but may well show him that there is a meaning (Frankl, 1969, ix). Frankl maintains that life can be made meaningful in three ways: (1) through creative work or what we give to life (2) through our experiences or what we take from the world and (3) through our attitude or the stand we take toward a condition we can no longer change such as incurable cancer (Frankl, 1967, 15).

In applying the principles of logotherapy, it is important to remember that the logotherapist cannot give meaning to a patient. Each person has the responsibility of finding that meaning which is unique and specific to their own situation. Frankl likes to use the analogy of an ophthalmologist who helps the patient to see more clearly. This may be done by either providing a lens so that the person may see more clearly or else by removing an obstacle such as a cataract which interferes with the patient's vision. In either case, it is the patient who must do the seeing. "The logotherapist's role consists of widening and broadening the visual field of the patient so that the whole spectrum of potential meanings becomes conscious and visible to him" (Frankl, 1959, 115). In the case of a terminal cancer patient, potential meanings might be living long enough to attend a daughter's wedding, finishing the writing of a book or giving an example of a noble attitude toward the dying process to one's family.

Another way of looking at the application of logotherapy to a particular patient's situation is that of Socratic dialogue (Frankl, 1967, 58). In this method, the logotherapist asks provocative questions and draws out answers from the patient. The assumption is that the answers are already contained in the mind of the patient, but are present in the subconscious. The role of the logotherapist is to ask pertinent questions and to bring up the answers from the patient's subconscious to consciousness. The purpose of this method, which Plato called midwifery, is to demonstrate that the answers lie within the patient and are not to be sought from the therapist or others. As Frankl points out, "meanings are found rather than given" (Frankl, 1969, 61).

The patient with incurable cancer faces a variety of problems. Some are physical (somatic), others are psychological (psychic), still others are psychosomatic. Some cancer patients struggle with religious issues (issues of faith in God) while virtually all terminal patients struggle with existential or what Frankl calls spiritual issues.

In the traditional, somewhat fragmented approach to care, physical problems are cared for by the physician and other medical personnel, psychological problems are addressed by the psychologist or psychiatrist and religious issues are the concern of the pastor or priest. Often no one addresses the existential or spiritual issues confronting the terminally ill patient.

To counteract this tendency toward a fragmented view of persons, Frankl has developed what he refers to as "dimensional ontology." In this approach, "the distinctive aspects of man are not viewed as separate elements or layers, but rather as dimensions or facets making up the individual" (Tweedie, 1961, 52). Frankl defines man as unity in spite of multiplicity (Frankl, 1969, 22). In logotherapy, man is viewed as being comprised of three dimensions–the physical (somatic), the psychological (psychic) and the spiritual (existential).

The physical or somatic dimension consists of the various organ systems such as the nervous system, cardiovascular system, pulmonary system, etc., which combine to maintain the functioning of the entire organism.

In the terminal cancer patient, the most common somatic complaint is pain. While logotherapy maintains that it is possible to find meaning even in the face of severe pain and suffering, Frankl is adamant in stating that this is the case only if the suffering is unavoidable. If the pain is avoidable, the meaningful thing to do is to remove its cause. "To suffer unnecessarily is masochistic rather than heroic" (Frankl, 1959, 117).

Dealing with unnecessary pain is one of the reasons the modern hospice movement has been so successful. For terminally ill cancer patients, the emphasis is on treating the symptom (pain), not the disease (cancer). When a patient enters a hospice program he/she realizes that the cancer is no longer treatable by surgery, radiotherapy or chemotherapy. This does not mean that "there is nothing more we can do for you" as some physicians still mistakenly tell patients. Pain and other symptoms can be controlled. In addition, the logotherapist can assist the patient in finding meaning even in the presence of suffering. Pain is the symptom cancer patients most fear. Maslow points out in his theory dealing with the hierarchy of needs, that lower needs (physiological and safety needs) need to be satisfied before one can deal with higher needs such as self actualization or meaning (Carlson, 1984, 648). In the case of a patient suffering from severe pain, the pain must be relieved before he/she will be able to discuss meaning. Modern methods of treating pain in a hospice setting with oral morphine given regularly or in severe cases using an intravenous morphine infusion will usually control even severe pain. At that point the patient will be more open to discuss meaning with the logotherapist.

In the last several years, the issue of physician assisted suicide has generated much discussion. The reason most terminal cancer patients give for requesting assisted suicide from their physician is lack of pain control. The hospice movement has taken the position that the answer to the problem of pain is not to be found with assisted suicide but rather with the effective control of pain. It is an amazing and sad fact that even with all of the modern methods of relieving pain available, many patients are still not receiving such care and as a consequence some are requesting assisted suicide.

Frankl discusses the issue of euthanasia or "mercy killing" at some length. He states "Must we not ask ourselves whether we are ever entitled to deprive an incurably ill patient of the chance to 'die his death,' the chance to fill his existence with meaning down to the last moment, even though the only realm of action open to him is the realizing of attitudinal values–the only variable the question of what attitude the patient, the 'sufferer,' takes toward his suffering when it reaches its climax and conclusion?" (Frankl, 1965, 46).

The term euthanasia refers to a good or easy death. In one sense, this has always been the goal of physicians–to provide a good death for their patients. This is expressed in the charge given to physicians in training–"Relieve pain, heal where possible and comfort always." In recent years, however, the term euthanasia has been used in a different sense. Proposals are now being made to legalize the termination of lives which are felt to be no longer worth living. Frankl addresses these proposals by stating that "it is not the doctor's province to sit in judgement on the value or lack of value of a human life. The task assigned to him by society is solely that of helping wherever he can. If patients and their near and dear were not convinced that the doctor takes this mandate seriously and literally, they would never trust him again. The patient would never know whether the doctor was still coming to him as a helper or as an executioner" (Frankl, 1965, 47).

While I agree with Dr. Frankl in principle and feel that it is never morally right for a physician to assist a terminally ill patient in committing suicide, I do think that the statement noted above is somewhat distorted. He seems to imply that it is the physician who is "sitting in judgement on the value or lack of value of a human life" and that it is the physician who is taking the initiative to be the "executioner." In reality, it is almost always the patient who makes the judgement that their life has no value or meaning and then implores the physician to assist him/her in ending this meaningless life. In most cases where physicians do comply with their patients' requests, I feel they do so out of a misguided sense of compassion for the patient–not as an "executioner." A more truly compassionate approach would be for the physician to use logotherapy to assist the patient in finding meaning in his/her life. If meaning can be found, suicide will no longer be an option.

Stanley Keleman in his provocative book *Living Your Dying* makes the point that most people live their dying as they have lived their lives (Keleman, 1974, 4). He distinguishes between "little dying" and "big dying." While we live, we are always breaking with the old and establishing the new. That is what he calls little dying. His hypothesis is that our little dyings are meant to teach us what our big dying (our final dying) may be like. Although we can know very little about death itself, we can know a great deal about dying since a pattern for dying is lived by each person during their lifetime through their "little dyings." Frankl makes a similar point when he states "The way a person dies, insofar as it is really *his* death, is an integral part of his life" (Frankl, 1965, 46). Kubler-Ross describes death as the final stage of growth. She states "Death is not an enemy to be conquered or a prison to be escaped. It is an integral part of our lives that gives meaning to our human existence. It sets a limit on our time in this life, urging us on to do something productive with that time as long as it is ours to use" (Kubler-Ross, 1975, x). Frankl couldn't have said it better!

How does a physician go about using logotherapy in a situation where the patient with an incurable illness feels his/her life is meaningless and no longer wants to endure the pain and suffering? Frankl uses the term "medical ministry" to refer to that aspect of logotherapy which deals with the treatment of somatogenic cases (Frankl, 1969, 117). He again points out that somatogenic cases are dealt with in logotherapeutic terms only when the somatic cause of the problem (e.g., inoperable cancer) cannot be removed. It is critical that priority is given to causal factors along with medical relief of pain and other symptoms. Once this is done, the treatment of the patient's attitude toward his/her disease and suffering is still possible and necessary.

Several different methods may be utilized in medical ministry. One is the "parable method." In this method, the medical caregiver relates a parable or tells a story which illustrates the point that no human being is exempt from illness and suffering (Frankl, 1969, 118). An example might be telling the story of Prince Gautama, who became the Buddha (Ross, 1956, 49). Gautama was the only son of a rich Hindu raja. His father expected him to become a ruler, but was afraid he might renounce his life and become a religious seeker. The father therefore did everything possible to protect Gautama from influences that would lead him away from the royal life. He especially wanted to protect him from knowing about the evil, suffering and unhappiness that existed outside the palace walls. Accordingly they attempted to make him feel that all life was happiness and pleasure and surrounded him with luxuries within the palace walls. In spite of his father's planning, Gautama one day took a drive outside the palace walls and saw four things that made a lasting impression on him. First he saw an old man and realized that old age comes to every one. Next he saw a diseased man and then a corpse lying by the side of the road. Finally he saw a monk with a very serene countenance. After this experience, he left the palace and began his search for meaning. He came to the conclusion that all life is suffering and that enlightenment can be gained only by renouncing the cravings that lead to suffering. In this way he found meaning. A story such as this can help the patient realize that all mankind suffers and that one can find meaning in spite of suffering.

Another method used in medical ministry is that of Socratic dialogue. Frankl tells the story of an old physician who consulted him because of depression following the death of his wife (Frankl, 1969, 118). The dialogue went as follows:

> Frankl: "What would have happened if you had died first, rather than your wife?"
>
> Old Physician: "How she would have suffered."
>
> Frankl: "Don't you see, that great suffering has been spared her, and it is you who have spared her this suffering; but now, you have to pay for it by surviving and mourning her."

Using Socratic dialogue, the logotherapist asks a provocative question, but the discovery of the meaning in one's suffering, in this case the meaning of a sacrifice for the sake of his wife, comes from within the patient. The meaning was there all the time–it only had to be drawn up to the level of consciousness by the therapist.

Logotherapy makes use of two additional methods or techniques–that of paradoxical intention and de-reflection. Since these techniques are generally not used in medical ministry, but rather in cases of psychological disorders such as phobias, I will discuss them later.

Given the variety of methods available in medical ministry, how does one choose the appropriate treatment in a given situation? Frankl states that the method chosen depends on both the individuality of the patient and the personality of the therapist (Frankl, 1967, 143). The relationship between the therapist and the patient is more important than the method used and is probably the most important factor in medical ministry.

The terminal cancer patient is confronted not only with physical or somatic problems, but also with psychological issues. Frankl considers the proper diagnosis of emotional problems to be the most important first step in psychotherapy. He states "He who distinguishes well, cures well" (Tweedie, 1961, 73). Frankl states that "every neurotic symptom has a fourfold root, being founded in the four basically different dimensions of man's being. Thus neurosis appears in four forms: as the result of something physical, as the expression of something psychic, as a means to an end within the societal field of force and finally as a mode of existence" (Frankl, 1965, 177). These are referred to as somatogenic, psychogenic, collective and noogenic neuroses. Logotherapy is most useful in the existential or noogenic form of neurosis since that is the area where man is most involved in decision making. In the physical (somatogenic) form of neurosis which is a result of physiological disturbances, there is very little room for decision making and accordingly logotherapy has little to offer.

Psychogenic neurosis is often the result of conflicts between drives and instincts and accordingly is amenable to the usual psychodynamic approach to therapy. Even here, however, logotherapy has something to offer in selected cases. For example, a terminal cancer patient may be constantly preoccupied in thinking about the manner in which he/she may die. As a result, he/she may not have any interest in their day-to-day existence or their responsibility to find meaning in life. This is somewhat analagous to the patient with severe pain whose attention is so taken up by the pain, that he/she cannot focus on finding meaning. In that situation, adequate pain relief is the answer. In the patients where excessive reflection or hyperreflexion is keeping them from thinking about the meaning of their life, the logotherapeutic technique of de-reflection may be helpful (Frankl, 1965, 253). De-reflection is intended to counteract the compulsive inclination to self observation. This can be achieved only when the patient's awareness is directed away from his disturbance (such as constantly thinking about how he will die) and redirected toward his unique meaning in life. The key to accomplishing this is self-transcendence. Frankl defines self-transcendence as that aspect of human existence which "is always directed to something, or someone, other than itself–be it a meaning to fulfill or another human being to encounter lovingly" (Frankl, 1978, 78).

The terminally ill patient has many fears. Fears, as opposed to anxiety, always have an object. These fears include the fear of pain, the fear of abandonment and dying alone, fear of losing control, concern about what will happen to one's family, fear of the unknown and in some, fear of going to hell. Anxiety is often referred to as objectless fear. Anxiety often begins as a reaction to a somatic condition or a psychological experience. Later the precipitating event may be forgotten and an anxiety neurosis develops. This often expresses itself as a phobia. This in turn often leads to anticipatory anxiety and a vicious cycle is established. An anxiety neurosis cannot be cured by the usual logotherapeutic methods such as Socratic dialogue. Logotherapy has, however, developed a special technique called paradoxical intention for dealing with cases such as phobias or obsessive-compulsive neurosis. In paradoxical intention the patient ridicules his symptoms rather than trying to run away from them (phobias) or fighting them (obsessive-compulsions) (Frankl, 1965, 259). Terminally ill patients would not normally be candidates for paradoxical intention since it would be difficult to convince such patients that they should ridicule their symptoms.

Terminally ill patients suffer from a different form of anxiety than that described above. Kierkegaard described anxiety as the struggle of the living being against non-being (May, 1960, 2). In his book, *The Concept of Dread*, Kierkegaard describes dread or what we might call existential anxiety as a general uneasiness before the undefined possibilities of life (Arbaugh, 1967, 160). This uneasiness results from the fact that man, because he has freedom, is able to choose between the possibilities which life offers, but because the outcome of his choices is always uncertain, he lives in constant anxiety.

Tillich defines anxiety as the state in which a being is aware of its possible non-being. He states "it is not the realization of universal transitoriness, or even the experience of the death of others, but the impression of these events on the always latent awareness of our own having to die that produces anxiety" (Tillich, 1952, 38). At its root, existential anxiety is the fear of the unknown and especially the fear of death. Although each of us is plagued by this type of anxiety to a greater or lesser degree, the patient who has a terminal illness suffers from this anxiety to an extreme degree. It is here that logotherapy can be very helpful.

Viktor Frankl saw and experienced this type of anxiety during his imprisonment in a concentration camp. Here the possibility of death was a daily occurrence. He describes life in the concentration camp as a "provisional existence." This same term might be applied to patients with an incurable cancer. Frankl states "it is a peculiarity of man that he can only live by looking to the future" (Frankl, 1959, 81). He noticed that those prisoners who lost faith in the future usually died in a short period of time. In such a "provisional existence," how does one maintain a faith in the future? The answer given to this question by Frankl is that one needs to stop asking what one expects of life and instead start asking what life expects of us. "Life ultimately means taking the responsibility to find the right answer to its problems and to fulfill the tasks which it constantly sets for each individual" (Frankl, 1959, 85). Taking the responsibility to find the right answers to life's problems is the goal of logotherapy.

In addition to existential anxiety, the terminally ill patient is also often confronted by existential frustration or frustration of the will to meaning. Such a patient, confronted by the tragic triad of suffering, guilt and the prospect of death in the near future, feels that his/her life no longer has any meaning. It is in such a situation that logotherapy is particularly helpful. The patient, with the assistance of the logotherapist, must be shown that life has meaning right up to their final breath. As previously mentioned, this meaning may be found by (1) creating a work or doing a deed, (2) by experiencing something or encountering someone, or (3) by the attitude one takes toward unavoidable suffering (Frankl, 1959, 115).

Frankl uses the term "noogenic neurosis" to refer to neurosis which results not from conflicts between drives and instincts (as is the case in psychogenic neurosis), but rather results from existential or spiritual problems such as frustration of the will to meaning (Frankl, 1959, 106). Such neurosis cannot be treated by the usual forms of psychotherapy such as psychoanalysis, but is more appropriately treated by logotherapy. Here the therapist uses methods such as Socratic dialogue or parables to assist the patient in finding that meaning which is specific and unique to his/her situation. In the terminally ill patient, this meaning often takes the form of developing a noble attitude toward his/her unavoidable suffering.

In addition to physical, emotional and existential (spiritual) problems, the terminally ill patient is also often confronted by religious questions such as "Where is God in all this suffering?" This raises the issue of how logotherapy is related to one's religious beliefs.

Frankl is insistent that "logotherapy is not a religious system per se. It neither aims to preach or to moralize, but rather to deal with the problems of meaning and value. It is not a system of ethics, but merely deals with the fact that man is an ethical being. The boundaries between psychotherapy and religion must be strictly observed and trespassing from one area to the other is strictly forbidden" (Tweedie, 1961, 148). Psychodynamic psychiatry often implicitly undermines religious beliefs by reducing them to mechanistic drives. Logotherapy does not avoid dealing with man's religious experiences, but maintains that the minister and the therapist have two different vocational tasks. The area of medical ministry which I previously discussed as being that aspect of logotherapy which deals with patients with incurable somatogenic problems is the area where the roles of the therapist and the minister often become blurred. Frankl states "Medical ministry is not ultimately concerned with the soul's salvation. Rather it is concerned with the health of a man's soul. And man's soul is healthy as long as he remains what he essentially is–in fact the very vessel of consciousness and responsibility" (Frankl, 1965, 277). The prime function of logotherapy is to bring to consciousness the spiritual (existential) factors of human existence along with the accompanying responsibilities. If the logotherapist is also trained as a pastor or priest, he/she must decide in which sphere he/she will deal with the patient (in the healing of the soul or in saving the soul) so as not to confuse the two vocational goals (Tweedie, 1961, 150).

Even though logotherapy has as its chief aim the task of helping the patient realize his/her unique meaning and values, the therapist should never seek to impose his/her own values or world view on the patient. He can help the patient to clarify or prioritize his/her values but ultimately the responsibility for choosing one value over another rests with the patient.

The patient who has just been informed that he/she has an inoperable and incurable cancer usually goes through fairly predictable stages in response to this news. These stages have been described by Kubler-Ross and consist of: (1) denial (2) anger (3) bargaining (4) depression and (5) acceptance (Kubler-Ross, 1969). It is important to remember that not everyone goes through the stages in this order nor does everyone go through each stage. The question arises: Does logotherapy have anything to offer in any of these stages?

In the first stage, the patient may make comments such as: "This isn't happening to me" or "my doctor must be wrong." Denial is a normal defense mechanism to an unpleasant situation. The physician or family member should neither agree with the statement nor should they attempt to break the denial. It is useful to think of denial statements as wishes rather than statements of fact. The best course of action is reflective listening to the patient. In time they will usually come to grips with the reality of the situation.

When the stage of denial can no longer be maintained, it is replaced by feelings of anger and rage. The patient will raise questions such as "Why me?" or "Why do I have to die?" In many cases the anger may be displaced onto medical personnel or family members. In what seems to be an unfair situation, anger is a normal response. The patient needs empathic and understanding listeners who can help the patient to vent his/her pent up feelings. No other therapy is needed.

Many patients will also go through a phase called bargaining. The term "bargaining" refers to the attempt to make deals with God or another person. The person may promise God they will go to church regularly if only God will let him/her live until their child graduates from high school or gets married. Kubler-Ross points out that the real significance of the bargaining stage is that the patient is beginning to face the fact that he/she is dying. This cannot be said of the denial or anger stages where the patient is either completely refusing to acknowledge the closeness of death or is displacing rage about the situation onto others. Frankl relates an example of bargaining on the part of a concentration camp inmate (Frankl, 1965, 137). The inmate states "I felt duty bound to my mother to stay alive. We two loved one another beyond all else. Therefore my life had a meaning–in spite of everything. I made a pact with heaven: if I should have to die, then let my death preserve my mother's life; and whatever I should have to suffer up until the time of my death was to purchase for her a sweet and easy death when her time came." It is important to note that in those patients who make bargains, the thing bargained for (in this case the mother's life) represents the meaning in the life of the patient at that time.

Most patients react with depression at some time during the course of their terminal illness. They often feel hopeless and helpless. One of the reasons patients become depressed is because of losses–either losses which have already occurred or losses which they anticipate in the future. In order to cope with these losses, the patient gradually begins to disassociate himself or herself from the world. This again is a fairly normal defense mechanism. It is during the stage of depression that logotherapy may be of real benefit to the patient. Even though depression in reaction to a life threatening and seemingly hopeless situation may seem like a perfectly normal response, the depression may be an indication of the lack of meaning in the patient's life. With the help of logotherapy, the patient can be taught that he/she has the freedom to take a positive attitude toward their suffering or in other words to actualize attitudinal values and thereby to find real meaning in their life (Frankl, 1965, 89). In such a case, the depression may be considerably improved and the patient may enter the acceptance stage.

In the acceptance stage, the terminally ill patient comes to terms with his/her situation and is at peace with himself/herself. In this phase, the anger, bitterness and depression subside. It is important however to ascertain whether the patient is truly at peace or whether the "acceptance" is merely resignation to a hopeless situation. If the latter is the case, logotherapy can still be of benefit in helping the patient reach "true acceptance."

As can be seen from this paper, logotherapy can greatly benefit the terminally ill patient. There are however many other modalities which can be used in conjunction with logotherapy. Logotherapy is a very "open" system and welcomes the addition of other therapies which may help the patient. We have already discussed somatic and psycho-therapies. Other modalities which may be useful include the hospice team approach, life review and the writing of both a will and a living will.

The hospice movement has revolutionized the care of the terminally ill in this country. The hospice team is composed at a minimum of a physician, nurse, social worker and chaplain. This assures that the patient is treated as a whole person. I feel that hospice care could be even more effective if one of the team members could be trained as a logotherapist. In this way the existential (spiritual) needs of the patients could also be addressed.

The life review offers the terminally ill patient an opportunity to integrate and make sense of his/her life (Birren, 1991, 6). Reviewing their past helps them to feel that their life has had purpose and meaning. A skilled logotherapist as a listener can facilitate the process of finding meaning by asking provocative questions during the course of the review.

The writing of a will enables one to clarify one's values. Thinking through carefully what one intends to leave to whom says a great deal about one's values. Similarly, the standard form for writing a living will provides a space for expressing one's philosophy of life. How one views heroic measures and life sustaining measures such as feeding tubes allows one to express to one's family how he/she views life and death. The living will allows one to express in advance his/her attitude toward dying which may have a profound effect on others not only during their remaining life, but even after they are gone. Their life can in this way be meaningful right up to the end–and beyond.

REFERENCES

Abrams, R. *Not Alone with Cancer*. Springfield, Ill.: Charles C. Thomas Publishers, 1974.

Arbaugh, G. *Kierkegaard's Authorship*. Rock Island, Ill.: Augustana Library Publications, 1967.

Birren, J. *Guiding Autobiography Groups for Older Adults*. Baltimore: John Hopkins University Press, 1991.

Buckingham, R. *The Complete Hospice Guide*. New York: Harper and Row, 1983.

Carlson, N. *Psychology–The Science of Behavior*. Newton, Mass: Allyn and Bacon, 1984.

Dollinger, M. *Everyone's Guide to Cancer Therapy*. Kansas City, MO: Andrews and McMeel, 1991.

Erikson, E. *The Life Cycle Completed*. New York: W. W. Norton, 1985.

Feifel, H. (1960) "Death–Relevant Variable in Psychology." In May, 58-71.

Frankl, V. *Man's Search for Meaning*. Boston: Beacon Press, 1959.

Frankl, V. *The Doctor and the Soul*. New York: Alfred A. Knopf, 1965.

Frankl, V. *Psychotherapy and Existentialism: Selected Papers on Logotherapy*. New York: Washington Square Press, 1967.

Frankl, V. *The Will to Meaning*. New York: World Publishing Company, 1969.

Frankl, V. *The Unconscious God: Psychotherapy and Theology*. New York: Simon and Schuster, 1978a.

Frankl, V. *The Unheard Cry for Meaning: Psychotherapy and Humanism*. New York: Simon and Schuster, 1978b.

Keleman, S. *Living Your Dying*. New York: Random House, 1974.

Kierkegaard, S. *The Concept of Dread*. Princeton: Princeton University Press, 1944.

Kubler-Ross, E. *On Death and Dying*. New York: Macmillan, 1969.

Kubler-Ross, E. *Death–The Final Stage of Growth*. Englewood Cliffs, NJ: Prentice Hall, 1975.

Lamerton, R. *Care of the Dying*. London: Penguin Books, 1973.

Leslie, R. *Jesus and Logotherapy*. Nashville: Abingdon Press, 1965.

May, R., ed. *Existential Psychology*. New York: Random House, 1960.

Nuland, S. *How We Die*. New York: Random House, 1993.

Rosenbaum, E. *Living with Cancer*. New York: Praeger Publishers, 1975.

Ross, F. *The Great Religions by Which Men Live*. Boston: Beacon Press, 1956.

Rossman, P. *Hospice*. New York: Fawcett Columbine, 1977.

Tillich, P. *The Courage to Be*. New Haven: Yale University Press, 1952.

Tolstoy, L. *The Death of Ivan Ilyich*. New York: Bantam Books, 1981.

Tweedie, D., Jr. *Logotherapy and the Christian Faith*. Grand Rapids: Baker Book House, 1961.

Walsh, T. D., ed, *Symptom Control*. Cambridge, Mass: Blackwell Scientific Publications, 1989.

Logotherapy and Adult Major Depression: Psychotheological Dimensions in Diagnosing the Disorder

Richard E. Close, MDiv, LICSW

SUMMARY. The diagnostic categories of Major Depressive Disorder (MDD) are expanded psychotheologically in a model which includes not only the biological and psychological symptoms but also those emerging in the dimensions of personal meaning and continued being. Frankl's Logotherapy assists in elucidating what a crisis of meaning looks like clinically and Tillich's formulation of the anxiety of non-being is adapted for describing the ontological crisis in MDD. A case study applies the model to one individual's approach to eldership. The ontological dimension is identified as the particular concern of Pastoral Counseling. *[Article copies available for a fee from The Haworth Document Delivery Service: 1-800-342-9678. E-mail address: <getinfo@haworthpressinc. com> Website: <http://www.HaworthPress.com>]*

Major Depression is a multi-dimensional mental disorder. Unlike other milder forms of depression, this disorder is of a more serious magnitude which once identified requires immediate medical and psychological intervention. Distinct from transient feelings of sadness, or a bout of the "blues," Major Depressive Disorder (MDD) is distinguished by its duration of two or more weeks ongoing and by a loss of

Richard E. Close, MDiv, LICSW, practices psychotherapy at Allina Medical Clinic in Cottage Gove, MN. He is a doctoral candidate in the DMin at Luther Seminary in St. Paul, MN.

[Haworth co-indexing entry note]: "Logotherapy and Adult Major Depression: Psychotheological Dimensions in Diagnosing the Disorder." Close, Richard E. Co-published simultaneously in *Journal of Religious Gerontology* (The Haworth Pastoral Press, an imprint of The Haworth Press, Inc.) Vol. 11, No. 3/4, 2000, pp. 119-140; and: *Viktor Frankl's Contribution to Spirituality and Aging* (ed: Melvin A. Kimble) The Haworth Pastoral Press, an imprint of The Haworth Press, Inc., 2000, pp. 119-140. Single or multiple copies of this article are available for a fee from The Haworth Document Delivery Service [1-800-342-9678, 9:00 a.m. - 5:00 p.m. (EST). E-mail address: getinfo@haworthpressinc.com].

119

interest on the part of the sufferer in most or all daily activities. Because these and the other clinical symptoms of MDD may be more difficult to distinguish in the elderly due to the physical manifestations of aging (such as a reduction in energy), or the isolation from family, friends, and previous responsibilities (feeling worthless), particular attention must be given to the diagnostic task in order to avoid misidentifying a clinically depressed elder. A review of the current *Diagnostic and Statistical Manual of Mental Disorders-Fourth Edition* (DSM-IV) will show that in its various forms and degrees of severity, the medical and the psychological dimensions of MDD including the two cited above are well-defined with enough specificity that significant relief and even cure of the distressing symptoms of the disorder have become possible. Medications increasingly target chemical imbalances in the brain resulting in much relief from the biological symptoms with significantly reduced side-effects. Correspondingly, verbal psychotherapeutic methods are becoming increasingly effective at identifying and treating the cognitive and resultant emotional symptoms of the disorder. However, as sophisticated as the treatment methods are becoming, they are limited by an incomplete diagnostic paradigm. Two critical dimensions have been left out, one assessing the experience of meaning, and the other that of being itself. Once these additional dimensions are integrated, a psychotheological paradigm is created which provides clinicians with a method for gaining a more complete diagnostic picture of MDD.

THE ROLE OF NATURE AND NURTURE

Medical science has established that MDD often has a bio-chemical and genetic etiology. Therefore it is no surprise that in some quarters of the helping professions there is greater emphasis on diagnosing and treating MDD exclusively as one might any other medical condition. This would include assessing such factors as the individual's family history of mental illness, life-style, and diet. Cure, defined here as symptom-relief, behavioral change, and a return to normal functioning, would be the goal of this approach since the sufferer is understood to be dealing with an internal biological imbalance, a force of nature. This could be described as the fundamental orientation of the naturalist perspective.

With the advent of third force humanistic psychologies there is an expansion of the understanding of mental disorders to include more comprehensively the variables of nurture in the development of mental health. That is, in addition to the biological "givens" of an individual's MDD, the nurturist perspective would encourage a clinician to consider the individual's past developmental experiences. Here the professional explores the past events, family messages, and interactions with others which were formative in both constructive and destructive ways. The individual's early socialization would be assessed including his or her experiences with key adult figures such as parents, teachers, religious figures, and other important people. Nurture may be construed in a broad manner since the most impactful or decisive events or relationships in the development of one's self-image and core beliefs may or may not occur within the family. However, a working assumption in this discussion will be that nurture (or the absence of it) is a major influence in the individual's mental and emotional well-being. It contributes not only to the foundation of his or her image of God and psychotheological worldview, but may also be a variable in his or her predisposition toward hope or despair. While the boundary between nature and nurture in the diagnosis and treatment of MDD is admittedly permeable, nurture will be assumed to take precedence in this development of an expanded paradigm for defining and diagnosing MDD. Matters of clinical practice will not be addressed in this discussion in favor of the diagnostic task. It is proposed that as sophisticated as the diagnostic methods presently are in the biological and psychological dimensions, equally developed methods in the noological (meaning) and ontological (being) dimensions are missing. While our current model increasingly answers questions regarding the nature of the biological and psychological variables in a given case of MDD, it does not articulate the noological and ontological variables equally and frequently operative in cases of severe depression.

The above claim can be qualified somewhat by the enriching contributions humanistic psychology has made to the process of diagnosis. In addition to understanding the medical and psychological dimensions of MDD and their consequences, Viktor Frankl's Logotherapy has gone further to ask about the individual's crisis of personal meaning and how that may be contributing to or ultimately causing a severe depression. He terms this a "noological neurosis" as contrasted with a "psychogenic neurosis" which describes the bio-psychological variables of MDD discussed above.[1] By adding this area of psychospiritual experience to the process of diagnosis Frankl provides us with not only an additional and important dimension for assessment but with a method to bridge the process of medical and psychological diagnosis into the realms of existential experience, and of ontology itself. By employing the work of Viktor Frankl and the Christian existentialist theology of Paul Tillich the paradigm for a psychotheological diagnosis grounded in the nurturist perspective may be expanded and deepened.

THE QUESTIONS OF PSYCHOTHEOLOGICAL DIAGNOSIS

A psychotheological diagnosis of MDD attempts to answer a fundamental question and its related subquestions in the face of the disorder: *What beliefs about life's meaning and one's essential being are operative in or contributing to the individual's severe depression?* That is, to what unquestioned core beliefs does the sufferer subscribe which form the foundation of his or her psychotheological worldview? And, consequently, how are these core beliefs self-destructive by serving to separate the individual from him or herself, significant others, and ultimately from a sustaining connection with God?

To respond to these psychotheological questions it is taken as axiomatic in this discussion that: (1) all people hold a psychotheological worldview by which they measure personal meaning and values, weigh their own worth, and explain suffering and loss, (2) this psychotheological worldview is in significant measure the product of one's past experiences including religious nurture which can, along with other formative influences, be identified, and (3) the most effective point of access to this personal psychotheological worldview is through the individual's cognitions. The shift from a psychological to a theological interpretation of MDD occurs by means of a cognitive assessment of the individual's psychotheological worldview and the resulting thoughts and beliefs. Aaron Beck, MD, has developed an effective method for doing this in his Cognitive Behavioral Therapy (CBT) and it is with this theory that the psychological to theological translation of the individual's beliefs will be conducted in doing a psychotheological diagnosis.[2] While a medical-psychological diagnosis remains primarily a descriptive task, expanding into a psychotheological diagnosis involves a dialogical task. That is, when a physician or psychiatrist is diagnosing a case of major depression, he or she is answering the question: *What does the individual have?* Is it, for example, an underfunctioning thyroid, or a reaction to a certain food or chemical? Is he or she feeling chronically lethargic due to a chemical imbalance in the brain, or sleep deprivation due to an organic cause? This is a process of elimination which needs to occur before proceeding to any psychological or spiritual hypotheses. Once this has been accomplished, and a medical depression has been identified, then the psychospiritual portion of the dialogical task may begin by assessing what Beck calls the "cognitive triad" of depression which includes: (1) how the individual views him or herself, (2) his or her experiences, and (3) his or her future.[3] These three areas constitute the substrata for the core beliefs which will ultimately point to the individual's psychotheological worldview. Once having delineated the biogenic and the psychogenic symptoms of the depression, the descriptive task is complete. To move to the dialogical task of making a psychotheological diagnosis Frankl's Logotherapy becomes central as the next question is posed: *What do the symptoms mean?*

THE CRISIS OF MEANING: THE NOOGENIC DIMENSION

In raising this question we are assessing the noogenic dimension. As Frankl develops it, in the noogenic dimension the helper explores the deep distress an individual feels when his or her will to meaning is frustrated.[4] That is, we experience, as Frankl calls it, an "existential vacuum," or a "frustrating inner void and desperate feeling of emptiness when our life appears to us to be without meaning."[5] This feeling results in a noogenic crisis which is caused by the " . . . unrewarded longing and groping of [man] for . . . an ultimate meaning to [his] life."[6] Treating this dimension is pursued through Frankl's method of Logotherapy. He defines the mission of the logotherapist in this way:

> The logotherapist is not concerned with treating the individual symptom or the disease as such; rather, he sets out to transform the neurotic's attitude toward [his] neurosis. For it is this attitude which has built up the basic constitutional disturbance into clinical symptoms.[7]

By defining the treatment involved at this level as an intervention with the individual's attitude rather than with discrete symptoms, Frankl postulates that such an attitudinal disturbance can over time result in clinical symptoms. The significance of this view for the psychotheological diagnosis of MDD is of paramount importance. The noogenic roots of MDD are here included with the biogenic and psychogenic dimensions in obtaining a fuller understanding of what is affecting the individual. In the noogenic dimension the crucial area assessed is the individual's *attitude toward* the disorder, or to put it another way, the individual's beliefs about his or her condition. This in turn is to be understood within the context of the individual's overarching sense of meaning in living. Once his or her depression can be understood in terms of his or her overall belief system concerning life's meaning and his or her purpose relative to it, then it is possible to proceed to the last question in the dialogical process which is: *How can the individual's crisis of meaning be stated in theological terms?*

To answer this question it is necessary to draw a distinction between two dimensions of MDD which follow from understanding the disorder in terms of the experience of personal meaning, and, in theological terms, the experience of being. MDD has often been understood to be predominantly, if not exclusively, biogenic and psychogenic in nature. With the introduction of the noogenic dimension the individual's lack of a sense of meaning or purpose in living emerges as potentially depressogenic. We could call this variable "existential depression" because a key component of the depression becomes identified with the individual's psychotheological worldview which assumes that his or her life is without a purpose. It is this core psychotheological worldview which requires a psychotheological diagnosis and intervention for healing to take place. Thus if the biological symptoms of MDD are a crisis of the body, and the psychogenic symptoms are a crisis of the mind, then the noogenic symptoms are a crisis of one's life purpose, a concern of the soul. What, then, is diagnosed when we shift to the task of translating MDD into theological terms? An answer to this is found in the DSM-IV criteria for both Major Depressive Episode and Dysthymic Disorder, a milder, chronic form. Although representing different degrees of severity of depression, it is significant to note that for Major Depressive Disorder the seventh criteria is "feelings of worthlessness,"[8] and that for Dysthymic Disorder the sixth criteria lists "feelings of hopelessness."[9] These psychospiritual variables are not elaborated upon in the DSM-IV because they are each embedded in a larger framework of biogenic and psychogenic symptoms (see the DSM-IV under "Other Conditions That May Be a Focus of Clinical Attention" [p. 685] where "Religious or Spiritual Problem" is cited as a potential area for clinical attention). However, Frankl's development of the existential vacuum is well-suited for understanding how feelings of worthlessness and hopelessness could over time develop into a clinical syndrome manifested as MDD. In fact it could be argued that both feelings of worthlessness and hopelessness manifested chronically over time and with sufficient intensity could provoke questions about one's continued existence and it is this crisis which moves the focus of a psychotheological diagnosis into the ontological dimension. That is not to say that the previous three dimensions of MDD disappear. They remain and still require treatment. However, theologically speaking, the individual's deepest (and empirically most elusive) struggle shifts to the question of whether or not to exist at all. This transition is evident in cases where a severe depression results in psychosis or suicide because both amount to a cessation of being either psychic or physical. Paul Tillich discusses this anxiety as ontological and it is here that the process of theological translation may begin.

ANXIETY AND NON-BEING

There is some risk in extrapolating only a few key concepts from the theology of Paul Tillich due to its highly organic and integrated nature. However, we are safe in beginning with his formulation of anxiety because what he describes it to be is a universal of human experience. By starting here we are not excluding any other equally vital corresponding categories.

A theological translation of noogenic depression to ontogenic must first retain its mandate to identify a crisis of the spirit, that is, a crisis of the very question of continued existence as an intentionally created, sentient, and relational being. This is why a psychotheological diagnosis in this dimension must be called ontogenic as opposed to noogenic. The crisis of life purpose, a dimension back from the ontogenic one, has more to do with a crisis of the meaning of one's life–a concern of the soul. Here, however, MDD has eroded the individual's capacity to address that concern and hence the question of the continuing life or being of the soul itself is provoked. Because this could lead to a physical or psychological ending of his or her life (which constitutes a unilateral undoing of God's intention in creating), this becomes a crisis of the spirit, that eternal part of us breathed into body and soul meant for meaningful relating with others and with God.

Tillich describes this existential anxiety as "the state in which a being is aware of its possible non-being."[10] In this state, especially when already depressed, this conscious awareness of the possibility of non-being is not merely intellectual. In fact, as Tillich points out, we prefer to feel fear rather than this profound possibility of non-being.

> Anxiety strives to become fear, because fear can be met by courage. It is impossible for a finite being to stand naked anxiety for more than a flash of time.[11]

This is why at the root of certain depressions, but particularly MDD, this ontological anxiety, this crisis of being, is to be found. In fact this ontogenic dimension occupies a unique place in the psychotheological spectrum because at this level of assessment an ultimate question is being posed to both the sufferer and the helper: *if this is all there is, why continue to live?* Here syndrome, symptom, sufferer, and helper are joined in a radical, if not unwelcome, equality. The question posed in this dimension is one which all humans potentially face, only the severely depressed elder for a host of biological, psychological, noological, and ontological reasons is much closer to it. At this point the diagnostic task leaves the purely descriptive realm. An ultimate question is posed requiring an enduring answer.

Thus far the exploration has progressed from the biogenic and psychogenic roots of MDD (the descriptive portions of the diagnostic task) to the noogenic and the ontogenic roots of depression grounded in the crisis of meaning (or soul) and being (or spirit). These latter two dimensions are described as the dialogical portions of the diagnostic task because the ultimate questions they pose for both the individual and the clinician necessarily comprise a dialog. Because the possibility of non-being is as real for the helper as for the helped how can an effective and objective psychotheological diagnosis of MDD be made in a way which generates a workable treatment plan? To answer this it is necessary to understand in greater detail what Frankl means by "meaning" and what Tillich means by "non-being" since these concepts adapted for the practice of pastoral counseling in particular are instrumental in moving a diagnosis into the theological realm.

VALUES IN THE CREATION OF MEANING

To understand meaning in the context of living, according to Frankl, we first need to appreciate an existential reality which serves as the ever-present backdrop for all of our hopes and strivings as meaning-seeking creatures. He describes this as the "tragic triad." No one, Frankl maintains, is spared from facing three commonly experienced realities in living and these are (1) pain as the reality of suffering, (2) death as the reality of our mortality, and (3) guilt as the reality of our human fallibility.[12] These three polarities of the tragic triad are the parameters within which all human experience takes place (including the natural need for meaning in living and the depression which results from a frustration of that need).

The experience of personal meaning as a measure for the quality of one's life can best be understood by considering Frankl's emphasis on the importance of realizing values in living because it is here that he equates meaning with spiritual health. In his book, *The Doctor and the Soul*, Frankl says that spiritual health may be defined as realizing or actualizing values which are of three kinds: *Creative Values* which are values realized (that is, brought into being) in creative action; *Experiential Values* which are values realized in peak experiences independent of any action; and *Attitudinal Values* which are realized in the attitude we take toward an unalterable fate.[13] It is through the actualizing of these three kinds of values that a life's purpose may be said to be meaningful.

Frankl points out that a meaningful life, one in which values are actualized, is not an abstraction. Each of us, he states, has a mission, a specific task "cut to suit" and it is in helping the individual in finding this task that professional healers can be most effective.[14] Spiritual health, meaningful living, and discovering one's unique mission or purpose are all anchored in the concrete business of daily life and suffering; consequently, the noogenic dimension has everything to do with MDD and the recovery from it. By grasping the importance of the realization of values in living, we come to see their role in diagnosing MDD in the noogenic dimension. For without the sense of purpose or mission in a concrete task, an elder becomes at risk of losing grounding in his or her life situation to such a degree that the resulting noogenic depression may provoke an increased vulnerability to, and a reduced ability to cope with, the deeper and more encompassing onto-logical anxiety related to non-being.

THE CRISIS OF BEING: THE ONTOGENIC DIMENSION

In continuing the process of developing an effective and workable treatment plan based upon a full psychotheological diagnosis of MDD Tillich's formulation of being and non-being provides a bridge from the noogenic to the ontogenic dimension of the dialogical task. In especially severe cases of MDD non-being may take the clinical form of a psychosis in which the former self of the individual is lost, or in suicide itself. However, professionals are likely to encounter the more familiar forms of non-being to which MDD can drive a despairing individual. Afflicted elders, for example (who often remain undiag-nosed), might "self-destruct" with chemicals, compulsive behavior, and other forms of acting out or passive self-neglect which can in effect leave them irretrievably damaged or altered to such a degree that the self which occupied that particular life-position is effectively gone.

As we move to the ontogenic dimension of the diagnostic task and begin to understand the clinical implications of the threat of non-be-ing, Tillich relies on the continued importance of the noogenic dimen-sion. Lack of a source and sense of meaning for severely depressed individuals may over time lead to the threat of non-being.

> We use the term meaninglessness for the absolute threat of non-being to spiritual self-affirmation, and the term emptiness for the relative threat to it.[15]

This anxiety moves into the ontological dimension when Tillich continues to say that the anxiety of meaninglessness "is anxiety about the loss of an ultimate concern, of a meaning which gives meaning to all meanings."[16] When rendered in psychospiritual terms, the anxi-ety a depressed individual experiences when their ability to find and experience a connection with God's creative purpose as the final source of all meaningfulness has been neutralized. The crisis of the spirit for the severely depressed elder who has deteriorated to this level of despair is not only found in feeling the erosion of the existen-tial vacuum, but in having entered into it without acquiring or retaining the capacity to have hope in the ultimately unbreakable connection between humanity and God. With no sense of personal meaning and no sense of an enduring source of it to which he or she could hope to return, the ontogenic dimension of the elder's MDD becomes fully manifest in the debate about continuing to live. The crisis of non-meaning has in this instance progressed to a breakdown of his or her *capacity* to have faith and the hope which stems from it. All of his or her remaining reasons for living come into question in the face of the possibility of non-being. A clinician might hear someone's despair in this dimension expressed in such phrases as "it's not worth it any-more," "I just want to go to sleep and not wake up," or "this must be a punishment." When he or she is speaking in terms of pain or frustra-tion they are still struggling in the noogenic dimension because they are aware of the potential to realize values in living but are frustrated in actually doing so. However, when an elder says things such as those quoted above containing themes of despair or guilt, then he or she no longer believes that there are values to realize in living *at all* and has thus moved to the ontogenic dimension.

It is essential to approach the diagnostic task in a systematic manner utilizing the best accepted methods available. This is especially true in the case of MDD because of its multi-dimensional nature and the ways it may be masked in elders. As stated earlier, the proposed paradigm developed here integrates usage of the DSM-IV, and assumes that a medical examination of the individual has been recently done. A good reason for this practice can be illustrated by considering endogenous depression which is a depression emerging strictly from the biogenic dimension, that is, from within the body.[17] To overinterpret this form of the disorder as anything more than that would be to assume psycho-genic, noogenic, or ontogenic symptoms where there may be none, at least none which are troublesome enough to require clinical attention. A complete psychotheological diagnosis must proceed with as much integrity and precision as a medical diagnosis, i.e., it should discern what the symptoms *are not* as accurately as what they are so that the right condition is being treated. The imperative to "first do no harm" is as applicable to a mental health professional as to a physician.

As mentioned earlier, the symptoms addressed in the noogenic and the ontogenic dimensions are not simply abstractions. It is proposed in this model that they are concrete, incarnated struggles inherent to the finite human condition with considerable power to transform or destroy depending upon when they are identified and how they are handled.

CASE STUDY

The following case is particularly well-suited for illustrating how the noogenic and the ontogenic dimensions of an individual's MDD are identified and diagnosed psychotheologically.

CASE HISTORY

Don (not his real name) was a 58-year-old who was seen for eight intermittent sessions in psychotherapy. He was married and had three children. Two of his adult children had left the parental home and the youngest was about to finish high school. Don had worked for a county government for close to thirty years as a court bailiff. He felt locked into this job and although he wanted to leave it he felt that he had to stay several more years to earn full retirement benefits. He described himself as unhappy in his marriage because although he saw his wife as a person with integrity, he acknowledged that he had not loved her for a long time and had considered leaving her. He spoke of feeling "down" all of the time with no sense of a potentially rewarding future. He had felt at times like dying although he had no actual plan about suicide. Don grew up in a conservative Protestant denomination in a small rural town. He was a "child star" in his local parish and went on to a small church-related college after high school. He majored in religion and planned on attending seminary in his denomination. He was well-liked and admired by his professors at the college and it was commonly agreed among them that he had the "right stuff" for the ministry. He had no dating experience when he met his future wife at the college when they were freshmen. They dated the entire four years at the school and it was assumed by family and friends that they would marry, which they did after graduation. Don disclosed that he had never told his wife about another woman at the college who had shown interest in him, a feeling which was mutual. Despite his interest in her he had never pursued a relationship with her for fear of what family, friends, and especially church officials would think of his morals. Not long into the marriage Don says that he rebelled against his church and cancelled his plans to go to the seminary. Married and at loose ends he took the job at the court because it was steady work and he felt he could do it without people wanting so much from him. He never envisioned it as a life's work. He had decided to seek treatment when he noticed that he was beginning to view his life to be as tragic as the cases he heard in the court room. Seeing his children grow up and leave home had also triggered painful retrospection and introspection for him, aggravating his depression.

THE BIOGENIC DIMENSION

The diagnostic interview began with the above history, and a DSM-IV diagnosis. Don met the majority of the criteria for MDD including the vegetative symptoms of hypersomnia, psychomotor retardation, and fatigue.[18] These symptoms had persisted well over the time period called for in the diagnostic criteria and he had no history of mania or psychosis. He was not taking any medications which could account for his chronic low mood. The insomnia and low energy raised questions about a possible medical condition and so he was referred to his doctor for a physical exam. After complying with the medical exam it was found that Don was generally healthy and that the depression was not strictly endogenous. He was placed on an anti-depressant medication in order to help him regain enough energy to participate in psychotherapy. This completed the assessment of the biogenic dimension.

THE PSYCHOGENIC DIMENSION

Unlike the symptoms of the biogenic dimension of MDD, the symptoms of the psychogenic dimension are based upon distorted and negative core beliefs and thoughts emerging habitually from a hopeless psychotheological worldview. These symptoms are seen frequently to include negative evaluations of the meaning of one's life, and the nature of one's very being. Self-esteem belongs to this dimension. It points to an important psychogenic variable in MDD. Psychotheologically self-esteem may be understood to mean the cumulative effect upon the individual's mood, self-image, and sense of worth of all that he or she through experience has come to believe about his or her purpose in God's plan for creation. In Don's case we can employ the categories of cognitive-behavioral therapy in analyzing his psychotheological worldview and core beliefs categorizing them according to Beck's cognitive triad regarding how Don views himself, his experiences, and his future. Beck states that the cognitive triad is fully defined as (1) *the individual's view of him or herself*, i.e., unpleasant experiences tend to become attributed to psychological, moral, or physical defects in him or herself, (2) *the tendency for him or her to interpret his or her ongoing experiences in a negative way*, and (3) *a negative view of the future* with the anticipation that his or her current difficulties or suffering will continue indefinitely.[19] Don was especially well-equipped to evaluate himself and his life in terms of the cognitive triad of depression due to his college major which in addition to religion had included philosophy. This background provided him with the concepts and vocabulary necessary to convincingly prove to himself that he was trapped in the over-examined life not worth living.

As our sessions progressed Don responded moderately well to the anti-depressant medication. His pervading sense that therapy itself probably would not help him subsided enough for him to begin revealing his deeply held beliefs. One of his core beliefs was that his current state of depression and dissatisfaction was the natural and unalterable consequence of his having left his denomination shortly after college. That, he stated, was the pivotal formative event in his life which sent him off of his path and into a loveless marriage and an empty career. As unfortunate as the outcome had been, he said that it was a just punishment for misusing his freedom of choice at that early age. In his psychotheological worldview, Don saw himself as guilty and hopeless. He viewed himself as morally bankrupt, a traitor to God who was punishing him with MDD. This was the core belief comprising the first part of his depressive triad. The others that followed were equally self-defeating. Don believed that his potential for a healthy faith-life had been ruined early in his upbringing and as a result even though he felt a strong yearning to reconnect with a more moderate faith community he was convinced that his damaged spirit would never completely integrate a new faith. Coupled with the first core belief described above Don sounded destined to interpret his current experiences in a negative way and carry them into his retirement years.

Regarding his marriage, Don had over the years told himself that his life would be better now had he pursued a relationship with the other young woman who had been interested in him in college. He had composed a detailed and elaborate narrative of the alternative life he would be living had he only married her instead. His career would be fulfilling, his love life complete, and his faith journey would not have taken the negative turn for which he was now being punished. This was an especially intractable core belief and he spent much of his time thinking about this fateful decision and how it was affecting him now.

The third major part of Don's cognitive triad of depression concerned his future. While he often sounded resigned to simply living out his "sentence" in his career and marriage, he acknowledged suicidal feelings when he was particularly in pain about his life or mentally exhausted from rehearsing them repetitively in his mind. He did not foresee a positive outcome for himself either in the short or long range. While he was never concrete about ending his life he often voiced a wish to "disappear."

By assessing the core beliefs outlined above we may assume that a useable inventory of self-defeating beliefs contributing to Don's MDD had been completed. These core beliefs had become habitual or engrained in Don's thinking. As psychogenic symptoms we may picture them as securely fitted lenses through which Don viewed himself, his world, and his future, habitually adding a depressive taint to any new experience. They are core cognitive distortions which Beck identifies as the primary target for change in CBT since left to their own devices the "distortions in thinking magnify until depression and hopelessness set in and take over."[20] Don's cognitive distortions had had many years to get established and elaborated. He had taken his life experiences and molded them to prove that he was being punished for choosing to leave his church, and for marrying the "wrong" woman, choices he had made over three decades ago.

THE NOOGENIC DIMENSION

Earlier in this discussion it was stated that the ongoing beliefs one holds about the meaning of one's life are the foundation upon which a psychotheological worldview is eventually constructed. In the noogenic dimension the diagnostic task becomes dialogical as the individual and the clinician enter into a conversation with the symptoms. In the current case Don has ascribed unquestioned validity to a set of self-defeating beliefs, giving them the power to pronounce his life misguided, "off course," and empty of meaning. His psychotheological worldview assumes a God who drops us into the world with a pre-established path which, if successfully discovered and followed, gives us a sense of purpose and fulfillment. However, should we choose incorrectly at any time along the way we can send our lives into meaninglessness and failure. From this position Don's potential to realize values in living was not only compromised, but essentially eliminated. He could not, for example, realize creative values because he felt immobilized in an empty marriage and a meaningless job. He could not participate in experiential values, as he had long ago distanced from friends and rewarding activities, making uplifting or pleasurable experiences unlikely or sparse. He could not exercise attitudinal values and adopt a new outlook toward his career history (such as ascribing value to his work because it made college possible for his children). This was impossible because he had convinced himself that they were the "wrong" children conceived with the "wrong" wife. One starts to get a sense in Don's psychotheological worldview of the underlying hopelessness which often characterizes MDD. For non-theologically oriented clinicians and psychiatrists this might be seen as the "end of the line" for Don regarding treatment. He was on a medication and had received supportive counseling. If hopelessness was still a problem it was not biogenic and further medical treatment would not be seen as potentially helpful. Major depression due to a perceived lack of meaning in living is not a medical condition. From a psychotheological point of view this assessment of the noogenic dimension of Don's MDD poses an existential question which is intrinsic to a crisis of personal meaning: Is this all there is? Frankl's formulation of the tragic triad serves as a paradigm for assessing the clinical significance of this existential question.

Don's experience of (1) *pain as the reality of suffering* was increasingly real to him as he lost the distraction of his children who were leaving home, giving him more time to experience his hopelessness. His experience of (2) *death as the reality of mortality* was especially evident in his fixation on his past as he kept himself intensively involved with the college youth he had been, holding himself accountable and culpable for a decision long since past as if to arrest time itself in an attempt to go back and do it "right." His deeply felt (3) *guilt as the reality of human fallibility* (a potential avenue to forgive himself) had turned itself around in his psychotheological worldview. Along with the official pronouncement of his former denomination, he declared himself guilty and condemned with no apparent avenue for appeal. Is this all there is? Noogenic depression asks this question when an individual looks at his or her past, present, and future and sees no overarching meaning or mission. A pastoral counselor is uniquely equipped clinically to confront this question and also to travel with Don into the last and most challenging dimension, the unique domain of pastoral counseling.

THE ONTOGENIC DIMENSION

The ontogenic dimension poses the greatest potential for healing but also the greatest potential for the helper to become ensnared in their own existential anxiety. To reach a severely depressed individual in the depths of the threat of non-being does not lend itself to the maintenance of a distanced, intellectual curiosity on the part of the helper. Nor is there room for would-be "saviors." To venture into the individual's noological and ontological crises the helper needs to be anchored in something beyond his or her own training, skill, and charisma. He or she must experience grounding in faith in a personally involved God who is the source of all meaning and being.

To begin a psychotheological assessment of the ontogenic dimension it is necessary to keep in mind that once MDD has moved beyond its natural limits in the noogenic dimension best interpreted with the categories of Logotherapy, the individual is likely to be getting serious about suicide or some other self-destructive course of action. The depression has evolved into the threat of non-being, which, as we have learned from Tillich, is something no one can bear in its raw state for more than an instant. This is a crisis of the spirit and it is best viewed that way because in this dimension the created being is contemplating undoing the act of the Creator by destroying itself. For Don much of this feeling and thinking was encoded in his passive remarks about "not waking up again" or letting an accident happen to him. Ironically, his early religious nurture was paradoxically both contributing to the desire to die and preventing his suicide as an unforgivable sin. It is here that a psychotheological assessment in the ontogenic dimension begins.

A psychotheological diagnosis may best be conducted if we accept as axiomatic that all people have a psychotheological worldview by which they define their life's purpose and the nature of their essential being. This psychotheological worldview is largely a product of life experience which can be identified and most readily accessed through the individual's core beliefs and their resultant thoughts and feelings. These core beliefs are assessed in order to determine how they are self-destructive in separating the individual from significant connections with him or herself, others, and God. A significant part of this task is to translate the meaning of the symptoms of MDD into theological terms and to do this they must be understood in light of the possibility of non-being.

Don's religious upbringing took place in a small, rural, and conservative Protestant denomination. There were clear lines drawn between the saved and the unsaved regarding denominations outside of this group. There were equally strict lines drawn between acceptable and unacceptable behavior and belief within the group. The expectations for young people entering its ministry were especially stringent and Don, being one of them, had come under close scrutiny since about High School. The image of God held by his church was one of an angry, punishing judge who watches our actions and monitors our thoughts looking for reasons to punish and exclude us. His was an adversarial image of God, one who was hard to please and more ready to condemn than to forgive. The congregation Don described was comprised of generally joyless people afraid of their clergy and of each other. The Bible was literally interpreted and from this an ideal lifestyle acceptable to God had been derived and required of its members. It never occurred to Don while growing up that this form of religious nurture might be oppressive. With an angry God at the foundation of his psychotheological worldview, a loveless marriage, and a closing career devoid of meaning were all to be expected and endured by one who had "betrayed" God and abandoned his call to ministry.

Don's psychotheological worldview was self-defeating and self-destructive. His ability to step back and rethink his core beliefs had been impaired. He was caught in a closed loop which was spiraling downward as each condemning belief reinforced the other. He was alienated from his originally hopeful inner self. His suffering was taken as proof that God was punishing him, or at the least had abandoned him to let the world have its way with him. Like many people, Don had found ways to cope with his depressive psychotheological worldview. He had spent years living under its oppression uncritically accepting the negative core beliefs stemming from it. For him, even if his life had become unbearable, it was only to be expected given his image of God. His alienation from others, and especially from his wife and children, testified to the power such a psychotheological worldview can have. As his MDD intensified in the face of his unrealized values and the shortening of time, it had moved out of the noogenic dimension into the ontogenic. A crisis of the human soul had become a crisis of the spirit itself. Without meaning or the future prospect of meaning Don had come to the question of non-being and was more vulnerable to it given the biogenic, psychogenic, and noogenic factors already affecting his ability to compensate. The consequences of his rigid religious nurture permeated his psychotheological worldview and image of God, as well as of himself, his circumstances, and his future prospects for happiness and meaning. He was alienated from a hopeful, sustaining image of God as well as from a healthy spiritual community in which to enrich his faith.

Don had started with the potentially helpful belief that we are all born with a unique and individual purpose in life. His particular church had rendered this belief toxic by ignoring the fact that even a unique purpose must be fulfilled in a finite world where no value comes to perfect realization. With no room for ambiguity or the possibility of redemption Don had been cut off from God as the source of all meaning. He had been mislead to believe that there was a "right" way to live out his unique purpose which left no room for deviation, life circumstances, or mistakes.

If there was no functional connection between the noogenic and the ontogenic dimensions of MDD then potentially any individual's struggle could be limited to and cured by interventions in the biogenic and psychogenic dimensions through medication and/or a standard course of psychotherapy. In Don's case this was not sufficient and a diagnosis assuming it was would be incomplete under the proposed paradigm. His MDD was affected by symptoms in all of the four dimensions.

There is, as we have seen in this case study, a dynamic connection between the crisis of non-meaning and that of non-being. Noogenic depression, if left undiagnosed and untreated, will naturally progress to an ontogenic one. Given that God has created us to be a hopeful people at all stages of the life span, finding our fullest being in realizing our unique purpose in the divine plan, a chronic sense of meaninglessness will evolve necessarily into a crisis of continued being. Such a crisis can be exacerbated in the elder years when the distractions of work, children, and homemaking begin to diminish.

CONCLUSION

Don derived visible relief from having the pain of his noogenic and ontogenic symptoms put into tangible terms. The biogenic and psychogenic dimensions were all too familiar to him and he had agreed to both medication and a course of psychotherapy which would begin with an assessment of his core beliefs and the resultant thoughts and feelings (standard CBT). He responded only partially to the medication and so the biogenic variables affecting energy and his capacity to participate fully in both thought and behavior change varied from session to session but had generally improved. By mid-therapy he was catching his self-defeating thoughts and enjoyed the sense of increased mastery he was developing in this area. He began to regain some hope in finding more congruent and meaningful activities outside of his work. He took a vocational interest assessment which continued to indicate a strong natural aptitude for some form of religious work. He started Spanish lessons at a local adult education program because he had always loved the language and wanted some fun. He thought he might start playing his trumpet again and planned to look for a good teacher and a community band. His marital dilemma was not significantly impacted by therapy in the eight sessions we met. He visited a more liberal Protestant church once and liked it. He planned to return despite the lingering sense that they were apostate.

With each step in this process Don reported that he was regaining lost ground and recovering parts of himself. He was no longer suicidal. Purposeful living was looking more possible as his fixation on his earlier self in college began to subside and with it the psychotheological worldview based upon God's retribution. He began reading theology and wanted to reconstruct his relationship with God. His skill at catching habitual, self-defeating thoughts had improved as he came to recognize them not as bonafide reflections of his true core beliefs but rather as symptoms in the psychogenic dimension.

This episode of treatment came to a conclusion at session nine. He committed to remaining on his medications and he had a plan of action to implement some of the positive changes he had identified for himself and his life. The beginnings of a transformation in his thinking had begun as he became more alive to the possibilities for increased meaning in his living. He began to identify, as Frankl would say, values he could create or experience which put a more benign coloring to his anticipated retirement. He was experiencing and cultivating the beginnings of a more authentic religious faith as he began to see past his despair. The process for a healing of Don's MDD in the ontogenic dimension had begun.

The currently well-developed biogenic and psychogenic dimensions of clinical diagnosis provide useful means for describing what is occurring in the human body and mind during an episode of MDD. These are the dimensions in which cure may occur. A psychotheological diagnosis, however, completes the clinical picture of MDD by adding in a systematic and intentional way the logotherapeutic dimension of personal meaning and the spiritual dimension concerning continued being.

NOTES

1. Viktor Frankl, *Man's Search for Meaning* (New York, New American Library, 1969) 112-113.

2. It may be argued that the variable of religious nurture is irrelevant when diagnosing irreligious individuals. However, the existential needs addressed by religion are universally relevant to all individuals and groups whether they adopt a theistic, organized religion or not. As a result the criteria of religious nurture or its absence remains equally significant in doing a psychotheological diagnosis. We cannot function without a personal theology, and indeed no one is.

3. A.T. Beck, *Cognitive Therapy of Depression* (New York: The Guilford Press, 1979) 19.

4. V. E. Frankl, *Psychotherapy and Existentialism* (New York: Washington Square Press, 1967) 55.

5. V. E. Frankl, *Psychotherapy and Existentialism* (New York: Washington Square Press, 1967) 53.

6. Ibid., 54

7. V. E. Frankl, *The Doctor and the Soul* (New York: Random House, 1955) 185.

8. American Psychiatric Association, *Diagnostic and Statistical Manual of Mental Disorders-Fourth Edition* (Washington: American Psychiatric Association, 1994) 327.

9. Ibid., 349

10. Paul Tillich, *The Courage to Be* (New Haven: Yale University Press, 1952) 35.

11. Ibid., 39

12. V.E. Frankl, *Psychotherapy and Existentialism* (New York: Washington Square Press, 1967) 29.

13. V.E. Frankl, *The Doctor and the Soul* (New York: Vintage Books, 1955) 43-44.

14. V.E. Frankl, *The Doctor and the Soul* (New York: Vintage Books, 1955) 54.

15. Paul Tillich, *The Courage to Be* (New Haven: Yale University Press, 1952), 47.

16. Paul Tillich, *The Courage to Be* (New Haven: Yale University Press, 1952), 47.

17. *Dictionary of Psychology Second Revised Edition* (1985), s.v. "Endogenous."

18. American Psychiatric Association, *Diagnostic and Statistical Manual of Mental Disorders-Fourth Edition* (Washington: American Psychiatric Association, 1994) 327.

19. A.T. Beck, *Cognitive Therapy of Depression* (New York: The Guilford Press, 1979) 11.

20. see Demitri, Papolos, MD and Janice Papolos, *Overcoming Depression* (New York: HaperCollins, 1992), 195.

Meaning in Long Term Care Settings: Victor Frankl's Contribution to Gerontology

James J. Seeber, PhD

SUMMARY. What are the sources of meaning in later life? Scholars and Biblical tradition offer explanations for this. Viktor Frankl has offered specific psychotherapeutic insights into human meaning that can be considered in the special case of nursing home elderly. However, meaning must take into account the several types of nursing home residents which include the terminal (comatose or active), the cognitively impaired, the cognitively intact but physically impaired, and the rehabilitation patient (short term). A list of potential sources of meaning to consider in preparing for ministry in nursing homes is presented. A ministry checklist of these sources in relation to resident types is included. *[Article copies available for a fee from The Haworth Document Delivery Service: 1-800-342-9678. E-mail address: <getinfo@haworthpressinc.com> Website: <http://www.HaworthPress.com>]*

INTRODUCTION

The question of meaning in the lives of older Americans has recently become one of conscious thought. Dr. Robert Butler's well-known volume, *Why Survive?*, published more than 20 years ago, frames the question that arises as we witness the elongation of human survival and the potential for keeping the body alive indefinitely by various

James J. Seeber, PhD, is Associate Director, Center for Aging, Religion and Spirituality.

[Haworth co-indexing entry note]: "Meaning in Long Term Care Settings: Victor Frankl's Contribution to Gerontology." Seeber, James J. Co-published simultaneously in *Journal of Religious Gerontology* (The Haworth Pastoral Press, an imprint of The Haworth Press, Inc.) Vol. 11, No. 3/4, 2000, pp. 141-157; and: *Viktor Frankl's Contribution to Spirituality and Aging* (ed: Melvin A. Kimble) The Haworth Pastoral Press, an imprint of The Haworth Press, Inc., 2000, pp. 141-157. Single or multiple copies of this article are available for a fee from The Haworth Document Delivery Service [1-800-342-9678, 9:00 a.m. - 5:00 p.m. (EST). E-mail address: getinfo@haworthpressinc.com].

extraordinary means. Experiments in health care and nutrition, ranging from late life hormone ingesting to caloric deprivation and with the frail elderly various treatment regimens including forced feeding by tubes can cause the vital functions to continue for almost unknown lengths of time. Furthermore, physiological researchers are now assuring us that we can expect to see the number of centenarians and the number of persons surviving for 120, or 130 years or more to rise equally sharply in the decades ahead. Modern scholarship has virtually muddled into the proverbial fountain of youth or some variation of it.

In the face of such dramatic change, questions of longevity and the geriatric issues of *how to* survive must yield to Dr. Butler's question, *why survive?* Such a question is not one of science with its penchant for factual reports, but one of religion with its capacity to help us find and attach meaning in life.

A number of scholars have reflected on meaning in the lives of older people. Moody, for example, cites the pioneering work of Carl Jung in terms of later life, "A human being would certainly not grow to be seventy or eighty years old if this longevity had no meaning for the species. The afternoon of human life must also have a significance of its own and cannot be merely a pitiful appendage to life's morning."[1] Such a position reflects an appeal to the genetic predisposition in the human species to survive. It implies a genetic meaning in human survival but does not satisfy us as to 'why'. Moody goes on to describe the last days of Larry Morris, a friend who came to live with the Moodys in his final days. While weakness confined him to one room, he regularly read the *New Republic* and was re-reading *St. Augustine's Confessions.* He bought a new computer for the Moody's children and wanted to understand how it worked. He had a spirit of inquiry which said, "I am still learning."[2]

Such behavior is not unknown among the frail elderly who are cognitively unimpaired. People have attended Elder hostel sessions until almost the end of their lives. At the retirement home where I am chaplain, I have seen persons actively involved in manor programs until their dying day. One retired seminary professor suffering with Parkinson's Disease expressed the desire (and intention) to write at least one more book on New Testament interpretation before he quit– actually he wanted to do three more, but was cut short of getting any of them finished. The point here is that he *intended* to write one or more books so long as he was able to focus on the ideas.

Biblical ideas, the traditions of the early church fathers and from at least the time of the reformation forward teach that long life is to be received as a "gift" or "blessing" from God, the all-wise creator.[3] In addition to understanding that long life is a blessing, something not fully accepted in a euthanasia-focussed society, long life was also understood in earlier times as a season of life for older people to be an example and model of faith for younger generations.

Steve Sapp and Mary Richards, in a workshop at the American Society on Aging Annual meeting in 1996, noted that *if* we all realize that "we are aging together," then a variety of common interests and a sharing of common efforts can occur between young and old. Such sharing would doubtless give meaning to the lives of older people, even as intergenerational life-styles with shared living tasks in many developing countries seem to enrich the sense of meaning and purpose among the elderly in those places.

Sapp and Richards cite the story told about a group of Jews who were fleeing Germany during the holocaust. Having to cross a mountain pass to reach safety, some of the older members began to tire and give out, asking that they be left behind rather than slow down the group. A number of younger people, fearing their own safety, were willing to agree. A wise younger person in the group, however, countered by saying, "we realize that you are tired and infirm, and that you just want to sit down and rest. But we have these young women with their babies, and they are so tired from carrying them this far. Will each of you take a baby and just carry it as far as you can before you give out? Then we'll leave you there." Everyone in the group made it across the mountains.[4] What does this tell us about *meaning* in human life?

FRANKL, LOGOTHERAPY AND AGING

Certainly the preeminent scholar of our time to deal with questions of meaning has been Viktor Frankl and his system of logotherapy. Frankl, a student of Freud, nonetheless held a strong existentialist view of human behavior. He was, for example, deeply persuaded, based on his observations in the German concentration camps where he was imprisoned, that human beings have a kind of radical freedom which no one is capable of taking from them. Building upon Frankl's insights, Fabry has observed,

> For our spiritual acts we are drivers; we make the decisions, take the responsibility, and accept the commitments. The motivation is meaning. We act from self-transcendence, for the sake of something beyond ourselves . . . To Frankl the human dimension is the dimension of freedom . . . not the freedom *from* anything, but the freedom *to* something, the freedom to take a stand toward conditions . . . Only neurotics, Frankl tells his students, misunderstand their experience as 'This is the way I have to be.' Healthy persons have the attitude of 'I can always change.'[5]

Such freedom might not seem a likely condition of older persons in long-term care facilities. Such freedom certainly would not seem to have been the lot of persons in the Nazi concentration camps. However, Frankl found in the camps, that some people retained a sense of fundamental meaning and survived the horrendous experiences while others succumbed to the devastating conditions and died. Those surviving were not always the younger or more physically healthy. From that puzzling anomaly came Frankl's camp-tested conclusion that *meaning* was the absolute key to understand human life and survival.

Meaning is not contained within us. Rather, it is to be discovered in life. While meaning is objective, i.e., outside of the self, the comprehension of it is individual and unique. Each person discovers it within his/her own life context. When the obstacles to seeing things clearly are removed, Frankl maintained, we tend to find our meaning in life readily and to give a creative response. Kimble, in summarizing much of Frankl's ideas about meaning, says,

> A person's life is never without meaning. It is a matter of refocusing and coming to a new understanding of the sources and shapes of those meanings. Logotherapy provides reorientation which helps older persons to view old age, not as a stage of stagnation and absence of meaning, but of new growth and development characterized by 'being' rather than 'doing' . . . Furthermore, it is a tenet of logotherapy that life's transitoriness does not in the least detract from its meaningfulness. Life holds meaning, whatever the circumstance, until the last breath.[6]

Frankl sees meaning as the human quality *par excellence*. He also treats meaning with such mystical respect that it parallels the role of empowerment experienced in the Holy Spirit in Christian thought. Ellor summarizes it well:

> Both the will to pleasure and the will to power derive from the will to meaning. Above the plane of human existence there is a level of supra-meaning that speaks to the human conscience concerning the meaning of each person's life. A person who believes in such a meaning lives a life open to the call of such meaning upon conscience, and is prepared to commit herself to a meaningful response to destiny.[7]

Frankl wrote that meaning, while it cannot be created, only discovered, can be found in three ways: (1) by creating a work or doing a deed; (2) by experiencing something or encountering someone; and (3) by the attitude we take toward unavoidable suffering.[8]

In another place he wrote that

> Life can be made meaningful in a threefold way: first, through *what we give* (in terms of creative works); second, by *what we take* from the world (in terms of our experiencing values); and third, through *the stand we take* toward a fate we can no longer change (an incurable disease, an inoperable cancer, or the like).[9]

These three aspects of meaning in human life–what we produce, what we experience and what attitude we take–are the broad background against which we will explore some operationally defined sources of meaning in long term care or nursing home settings. The sources discussed derive from observation over many years' experience as a chaplain and sociologist.

In examining meaning in long-term care settings, it is important to take account of the mixed population that resides in most nursing homes. Mor, Banasek-Holl and Zinn[10] discuss the move toward specialization in nursing home care that became widespread in the 90s. Many homes feature special (1) Alzheimer's units, (2) subacute care and/or rehabilitation care, (3) AIDS units, (4) hospice units, or (5) Medicare treatment units. This has been well-documented in several reports. In a separate article, Petrisek and Mor studied the proportion of homes that have either hospice patients or special hospice units.[11] Health Care Financing Administration (HCFA) statistics taken from home inspections done between July, 1995 and April, 1997 show that about 30% of all homes have at least one hospice resident and about 4.25% of all facilities have 5% or more of their residents on the Medicare hospice program. Furthermore, while a majority of facilities with special hospice units had Medicare hospice residents, all did not. Among homes without hospice units, about 29% had one or more hospice resident.[12] The expansion of nursing homes to include formal hospice care is developing quickly. As with most specialization units in nursing homes, those facilities most often moving into the hospice field tend to be for-profit and/or larger facilities.

In a related article, Rosalie Kane discusses the varied types of residents in nursing homes today. If "diversity" describes the older population in general, it also describes nursing homes well. Kane argues that all who work within these environs need to be far more sensitive to the mix of persons and their differing needs. One size does not fit all![13]

Kane sets forth a half dozen categories of residents and calls for differential treatment and response to each of them. The Typology Table of Nursing Home Residents represents an adaptation of her categories. Kane's six divisions can be grouped into three in terms of the master variables that must be noted: A. Terminal condition (comatose and hospice) persons; B. Cognitively impaired (Alzheimer's, both early stage and advanced); C. Cognitively intact (transitional persons anticipating discharge, and long term residents).[14] In Table 1, the categories for relevant treatment are divided into five groups. There are differences in terms of meaning issues across the five groups, however, so they are distinguished in the table. Also, there are common though not universal patterns regarding who is expected to take the formal lead in offering spiritual care in each case. For example, for comatose persons, the family is the care recipient and the family pastor (if there is one) is usually the lead provider. However, with long term cognitively impaired residents, the resident and/or the family is the care recipient and the institutional chaplain is the lead person.

SOURCES OF MEANING–MAJOR VARIABLES

The sources of meaning noted and discussed are not exhaustive, but are based upon impressions in 15 years as a long term care chaplain. A checklist of these factors by types of LTC resident is as follows:

Sources of Meaning in Long Term Care

1. Maintains Relation with people outside.
   a. Friendship Network
   b. Family contact

2. Control of daily routine

3. Privacy

4. Intimacy/Sexual express

5. Intellectual Stimulation

6. Support for Self-identity:
   a. Life Purpose (Reker)
   b. Will to meaning (Reker)

7. Reinforces Ethnic/Cultural habits

8. Sense of security re.
   Health/well-being

9. Optimism:
   a. Anticipates future events
   b. Confidence they will occur

10. Environmental Quality
    (Eden Alternative, etc.)

11. Rituals/Relig. Observnce:
    a. Collective
    b. Individual

*This form may be copied and used freely. Please contact the author with suggestions/questions.

TABLE 1

TYPES OF LONG TERM CARE PATIENTS*

		Comatose (Hospice)	Terminal (Dementia)	Advanced Impaired	Cognitively Intact	Rehab Pt. Short Term
Spiritual	Recipient	Family	Family/Patient	Family	Family/Patient	Patient
Care	Lead person	Pastor	Chaplain	Chaplain	Chaplain	Chaplain

Maintaining Relations with Family/Friends Outside the Facility

The importance of having family and friends and of regular contact with at least some of them has been well documented in numerous studies over the years. Numerous studies have documented the value of having a 'confidant' for survival in later years. It is clear that the ability to maintain contact with long time friends and family members is generally helpful but varies by the type of patient. Most persons with dementia lose all but the most immediate family as social contacts. Many people have no idea how to relate to a person that repeats themselves over and over or who doesn't remember the name of longtime friends, etc.

Normal ways of maintaining ties with friends are often problematic in institutional settings. Visitors feel they cannot drop in at any time; telephones are not easily available though in-room phones are becoming more common; residents are not free to come and go from the homes though on occasion some can go out with family for special occasions; letter writing too can be problematic for persons with arthritis and/or may take a higher level of extended concentration than many residents can offer. All in all, nursing home admission is often followed by significant social isolation. Added to that is the reality that today's nursing home residents are increasingly very frail when they enter the home and many experience serious problems trying to maintain what would be normal social ties in their homes. Changes in policies and practices on a range of matters and devices such as user-friendly computers with very large screen print may be a partial solution for those who wish to write letters.

Do friendships in institutions mean as much as former friendships did? In an in-depth study of nursing home social patterns, Seeber[15] found that: "though quite a bit of visiting takes place among those able to do so, without exception, all patients considered the friendship ties as less intimate and more general than those they had shared outside."[16] This lack of closeness suggests "the critical importance to the patient of the disengagement from meaning or what could be called the loss of identity."[17] Of twelve patients in Seeber's study sample, five were fully 'identity disengaged' and were all notably depressed; four had found new friendships and social routines within the institution and were socially satisfied; three others were able to maintain outside friendships–two via letter writing and one vicariously through daily reports from her spouse who kept her up on the neighborhood gossip.[18] Family ties are also variable in nursing homes. On the one hand, many persons are in nursing homes because they have no family to weave the support network needed to remain in the community. On the other hand, several studies have shown the myth of families abandoning the elderly in later life[19] or after they enter a nursing home to be just that–a myth!

The value of family and friendship ties is seen in Reker's study of depression.[20] Nearly 20% of the variation among nursing home residents predicting who was depressed was determined by social resources (including frequency of contact with family and friends).

Control of Daily Routine

Another major source of meaning that has been considered from the negative side of 'learned helplessness'[21]–a quality endemic to institutional settings–is when persons have a feeling of efficacy or control over much of daily life. On the positive side, residents who can "live meaningfully, exercise choice, and maintain social ties and familiar lifestyles as much as possible"[22] are far more likely to be satisfied. The sense of efficacy has been found to affect survival rates as well as satisfaction. In one nursing home, a woman was seen at lunchtime to be sitting in her wheelchair quietly weeping. When asked by an aide what was wrong, all she replied was "butter on my cornbread; I don't like butter on my cornbread." Her sense of control over her life had declined so far that she could not even affect having butter on her cornbread although she had told staff on numerous previous occasions that she did not like butter on her cornbread!

Privacy

Privacy is very problematic in nursing homes. The lack of privacy and respect for the resident is a continual reminder that a nursing home is not a home. As Kane has suggested based on a number of general studies, "Institutions are poor living environments."[23]

One strong-willed old woman in a home in the Midwest created an uproar by verbally "throwing staff out" of her room on several occasions during her first few days in the nursing home. They entered without knocking; an aide went directly to her closet and began to go through her clothes without asking permission, and they disturbed her when she preferred to take an afternoon nap. She informed them that this was her room by god; she was paying their salaries and they had best remember who was the resident and who was the staff there! After that, she received a high degree of autonomy and deference from all concerned. Whether she received a diminished quality of care in the longer term is not known.

Intimacy/Sexual Expression

One aspect of privacy that has received limited attention in nursing home environs is the desire for privacy to allow intimacy and sexual expression between persons. Loneliness is endemic in nursing home settings. The opposite of loneliness, however, is not activity. It is intimacy. The dilemma is that stereotypes of frail elderly cause many homes to assume that intimacy is either unnecessary or is inappropriate at that age. Nothing could be more incorrect. Expressions of love and affection and feelings of closeness are without a doubt some of the strongest motivations for living and sources of meaning to all people, yet frail elderly are often denied such affection or closeness because of their age and stage in life. Some homes have adopted "sexual expression codes"[24] spelling out the rights and conditions of privacy for spouses or other "couples" to have private times together. This sensitivity, along with practical arrangements to implement it in a congregate living setting, offers at least a hint that nursing home residents may be considered human after all. A recent graduate of the Geriatric Pastoral Care Institute (GPCI) told about a yearlong struggle to allow an older couple in her nursing home to get married. There were reservations from every side–administration, families, etc., except from the couple themselves. The couple was ultimately married, with the blessing of all parties, thanks in no small part to the advocacy and mediating role of the chaplain between all parties!

Intellectual Stimulation

Many residents are cognitively unimpaired and living in environments where they mingle with seriously demented neighbors in a setting where activities are often geared to keeping people busy who have limited cognitive skills. Kane noted that cognitively unimpaired residents have different needs than Alzheimer and other types of residents. Some homes have regular intellectual forums and classes. Some chaplains hold Sunday school classes or Bible Study groups with residents. One home in California in cooperation with the local adult school program hosts classes in their facility. Classes in California

History and other topics are attended by townspeople and also by residents. The opportunity to mix with others in a common learning experience is highly satisfying to some of the residents. One recent GPCI graduate led a Life Review course in the nursing center of his retirement home. Others have led Spiritual Autobiography classes.[25] These and one-on-one times of stimulation are very valuable to cognitively intact elderly in the homes.

Support for Self-Identity

In examining the primary influences that act as deterrents to depression among both community-dwelling and institutionalized elderly, Reker tested several existential variables as well as the traditional factors of social support and physical health. In administering a questionnaire to both subsets of subjects, Reker examined personal meaning in life by asking about life goals and mission, sense of identity, and a sense of order as well as future expectations. He found overall that the institutionalized were more depressed, had a lower sense of meaning, and perceived themselves as having less choice and responsibleness than the community-dwelling elderly. He found institutional females significantly more depressed than males. The amount of variation in expected depression was explained by numerous variables. Among these, the existential variables including life purpose and will to meaning questions explained a respectable 15% of the variation. Personal meaning was the most significant of the existential factors but each had some value.[26] Given the radical dislocation and social isolation entry into a nursing home causes most people, it is easy to see why depression would run higher among institutionalized than among community-dwelling people. The question for professionals in these institutions is what can be changed to enhance a sense of life purpose and a sense of personal order and personal identity among residents?

Reinforces Ethnic/Cultural Traditions

As persons advance in years, many tend to re-identify with their roots and to hold fast to those ethnic qualities they understand. Institutions that can assist older persons, minority as well as majority groups in homes, to embrace and celebrate their cultural and ethnic heritage will both strengthen personal identity (as noted above) and will enrich the lives of residents.

Sense of Security Regarding Health/Well-Being

As Kane has noted,[27] persons with some cognitive impairment need to feel safe in their environment and secure regarding who will take care of them when health crises arise. There is a safety in routine and while the more alert may chaff at repetitive schedules, the cognitively impaired find comfort in unchanging routines that are not very complex and that include cues (physical or social) for orientation. Having traditional altar furnishings for worship services, for example, immeasurably improved the meaning worship had for the cognitively impaired in the care center where the author was chaplain.

Optimism

Some scholars have suggested that there is no future orientation or at best, a diminished future view among frail elderly. Reker found those who lacked a future orientation were more depressed than those who both had desirable events they looked forward to and expectations that those events would happen.[28] Certain milestones seem to carry extra meaning. One woman in a nursing home spent several months anticipating a 100th birthday celebration and the party her family had planned with her for that occasion. She not only relished the day when it came, but remembered it fondly for many months afterward. She was cognitively unimpaired and the birthday was a day of renewal of friendships and family ties. Gubrium has noted that many in institutional settings gauge the passing of time by the anticipation of approaching events which have some degree of meaning–meals, movietime, bingo, etc. How important it is for family or friends to honor announced plans to visit residents as the cognitively unimpaired especially look toward such events.

Liturgical seasons seem to help residents gauge the passing of time and to anticipate upcoming events. Even residents with significant dementia can join in anticipation of Christmas as they see the decorations and hear the music of the season. Much the same can be true of other liturgical seasons by use of vestments and songs or appropriate customs that lead persons to prepare appropriately. Friedman reminds us that religious ritual in the life of nursing home residents helps to celebrate significant time and to offer continuity both within their own lives and a tie to the larger community of faith.[29] Easter, the celebration of communion during Holy Week among Christians, observing

Rosh Hashanah and other holy days among Jews and Ramadam among Moslems helps to place life in a context of continuity.

Environmental Quality

Dominated by a hospital-like "medical model," Kane has noted how inhumane many nursing home settings are. A movement to re-humanize the nursing home is the Eden Alternative.[30] Introducing touches of a home-like atmosphere and re-training staff to a less rigid medical care model allows persons to feel a little bit more "at home." Examples exist of the physical designing of facilities for a more familiar feel as in the case of the "Main Street" arrangement of the central lobby for the Passavant Retirement Home in Pennsylvania. Changing an institutional environment, especially one that is regulated by multiple boards and state agencies, is not easy, and the role of advocate and mediator by spiritual care leaders can be very helpful in implementing such change.

Religious Rituals

There has been little careful research to indicate the direct benefit of collective worship experiences with long term care residents, but impressions suggest that thoughtfully done worship times are very beneficial. Comments by nurses in nursing homes suggest that residents who are restless or have dementia seem to be calmer after worship than before. Residents themselves often verbalize how much the regular worship times mean to them. At the manor where the author served as chaplain, residents, knowing it was nearly time for the worship service, would wheel themselves to the area where worship was to be held, and many coming by later would enter the worship service unbidden. General studies of religion have suggested that one of the functions religion perennially has served is that of comfort and meaning in the face of life's dilemmas. Certainly moving into a nursing home poses a major dilemma for many elderly.

Collective rituals must be sensitive to what is familiar and supportive with the "congregation" being served. A retired "preacher" volunteered to come to a nursing home weekly to lead a gospel service. He brought a boom box with country "hymns" that he alone knew and spent half an hour crudely wailing the songs in the face of the residents who had been wheeled in to hear him. Other than clapping in rhythm on one or two of the songs, there appeared to be no interaction between the people and the service at any time. The preacher left instead of staying to visit one-on-one during a refreshment time that followed the gospel service.

Individual pastoral visits by clergy or trained lay members from the church or synagogue to which persons are related can help maintain a bond with the religious community as well as help residents to share some of their life concerns with a caring person. The effect of this can be to help bring God near in a very personal way for residents. The cognitively intact nursing home resident has time to read familiar scripture or religious material–either large print materials or audio cassettes of the Bible are readily available–and to reflect on her/his faith journey as well as time to pray for himself/herself, and for her/his family and loved ones as well as other concerns.

A BRIEF DIGRESSION:
COMMUNITY-BASED LONG-TERM CARE

Although this session is chiefly about meaning in long-term care institutions, let me treat "Long Term Care" very broadly for a moment and focus on "community-based long-term care." There are two general models that might be lifted up–the Program for All-Inclusive Care of the Elderly (PACE) Model and the Community-Home Health/ Supportive Services Model.

An experiment pioneered through the On-Lok Senior Center in San Francisco led to nationwide model projects called the PACE. Fifteen different projects were funded through HCFA (Health Care Financing Administration) in the mid-1990s to learn whether community care for persons that qualified for nursing home care would do as well and/or cost less to administer in the community. A GPCI alum, Sr. Rosalie Orr at Providence Health Systems in Portland, was a participant in one such model project.

PACE consolidates care and financing to meet the whole range of needs for nursing home eligible persons. The program emphasizes (1) maximum independence of persons, (2) for the frail elderly, (3) offering comprehensive services, (4) management of all care services by an interdisciplinary team (including chaplains), (5) financed through a flat contract rather than a fee-for-services system. Early analysis of the projects suggests that costs run 10-15% below comparable care costs in nursing home settings.[31] Enrollees also had significantly shorter hospital stays, adding further to the savings. In Portland a significant number of the PACE participants were living in foster homes since Oregon has a very aggressive program for elder foster care. PACE is a promising program in searching for an alternative to nursing home care.

From the spiritual care perspective, where does/would a chaplain fit into this type of program? In the Portland model project, the Catholic hospital system included chaplain services at the PACE center, but what about other settings where spiritual care might not be as visible? Through seeking to serve this frail elderly population, a religious program each day with the "gathered community" could be included. Home visits and the availability of spiritual care in the case of death and dying might prove valuable. Religious leaders need to be aware of how frail older people are being cared for in our cost conscious society and to access and be part of the system of care.

The other concept of "community-based long-term care" is in fact being provided by home health agencies around the nation. Federal funds are being reduced for this quickly expanding service and local agencies are cost conscious about utilizing personnel so that nurses have enough funds for frequent contacts. However, pastors/chaplains who are available as associates without pay (or better, paid by a local consortium of congregations to do spiritual care in home-healthcare programs) could be helpful as both liaisons between local congregations and the service as well as mediators with families. In California recently a home health agency experienced a severe family crisis as to who was going to provide personal care at home for a very ill gentleman, his adult daughter or his (new) wife. After repeated standoffs with the visiting nurses, the family's priest was asked to intervene. He met with some of the family, softened the attitudes, and helped the consulting doctor to convene a family conference with all parties present to agree on how dad was to be cared for. The priest's influence doubtless helped to get the door opened to a successful family conference.

In St. Paul, MN, a major hospital, as part of its after-care program following discharge, provides home health and support services and a chaplain is part of the team, going into the homes on request to help strengthen the individual and family support following hospital stays.[32] As the decentralization of health services continues and expands, there will be greater need for chaplains/pastors to find creative ways to fit into the system of care. The liaison function with parish clergy will be increasingly valuable, and also the advocacy and mediating function (as noted above) will be needed. Long Term care is not what it used to be.

CONCLUSION

Meaning-making in institutional environments is a complex process. This discussion has been focused on what the religious or spiritual care leader needs to know and consider in providing adequate spiritual care to complement those things that help frail older persons find meaning while living in a nursing home or similar setting. Frankl understood that no one can give meaning to another and that the heart of the meaning lies outside of the person waiting to be discovered. The long-term care resident must want to find meaning, and hopefully, the spiritual care staff will be an ally in this process. It is critically important that the differences in types of need between different residents in facilities be taken seriously and that a team approach be followed when assisting the resident in his/her search for a life with meaning.

NOTES

1. Carl Jung, *Modern Man in Search of a Soul* (New York: Harcourt and Brace, 1936), 109.

2. H. R. Moody, "Meaning and Late-Life Learning," Keynote address, International Association of Universities of the Third Age (Finland, August, 1994), 6.

3. K. Brynolf Lyon, *Toward a Positive Theology of Aging* (Philadelphia: Fortress Press, 1986).

4. Mary Richards and Steve Sapp, "Finding Meaning and Hope in a Time of Conflict: The Role of Religion," Workshop presented at American Society on Aging (1996), 13-14.

5. J. B. Fabry, *The Pursuit of Meaning* (San Francisco: Harper and Row, 1968), 19.

6. Mel A. Kimble and James W. Ellor, "Logotherapy: An Overview," paper in American Society on Aging and National-Louis University, 1991.

7. James W. Ellor, "Meaning in Later Life," *Seasons: The Interfaith Family Journal* 12, no. 2 (1995): 12.

8. Viktor E. Frankl, *Man's Search for Meaning* (New York: Washington Square Press, 1959), 133.

9. _____, *The Doctor and the Soul* (New York: Vintage Books, 1965), xii.

10. V. Mor, J. Banasek-Hall, and J. Zinn, "The Trend Toward Special Institutions in Nursing Care Facilities," *Generations* 14, no. 4 (1995-1996): 25.

11. A. C. Petrisek and V. Mor, "Hospice in Nursing Homes: A Facility-Level Analysis of the Distribution of Hospice Beneficiaries," *The Gerontologist* 39, no. 3. (1999): 279-290.

12. Ibid.

13. Rosalie Kane, "Transforming Care Institutions for the Frail Elderly, Out of One Shall Be Many," *Generations* 14, no. 4 (1995-1996): 62-68.

14. Ibid.

15. James J. Seeber, "The Nursing Home Patient: A Look at His Life Situation and Needs" (diss., Claremont School of Theology, 1972).

16. Ibid.

17. Ibid.

18. Ibid.

19. H. Lopata, ed. B. Neugarten. *Middle Age and Aging* (Chicago: University of Chicago Press, 1968).

20. Gary T. Reker, "Personal Meaning, Optimism, and Choice: Existential Predictors of Depression in Community and Institutional Elderly," *Gerontologist* 37, no. 6. (1997): 709-716.

21. R. Kane, E. Langer, and J. Rodin, "The Effect of Choice and Personal Responsibility for the Aging," *Journal of Personality and Social Psychology* 34 (1976): 191-198; S. Mercer and R. A. Kane, "Helplessness and Hopelessness among the Institutionalized Aged: An Experiment," *Health and Social Work* 4,(1979):90-116; R. Schulz, "Effects of Control and Predictability on the Physical and Psychological Well-Being of the Institutionalized Aged," *Journal of Personality and Social Psychology* 33 (1976): 563-573.

22. Kane.

23. Kane.

24. For information: Rev. Willard Ressler, Chaplain, Hillcrest Homes, LaVerne, CA.

25. R. L. Morgan, *Remembering Your Story: A Guide to Spiritual Autobiography*, (Nashville: Upper Room, 1996).

26. Kane.

27. Kane.

28. Reker.

29. D. Friedman, "Spiritual Challenges of Nursing Home Life" in *Aging, Spirituality and Religion: A Handbook* ed. Mel Kimble et al. (Minneapolis: Fortress, 1995) 365-366.

30. For more information, Eden Alternative, 742 Turnpike Rd., Sherburne, NY 13460: web site: www. edenalt.com.

31. Report on PACE in *Benjamin Rose Institute Newsletter* Fall, 1997. 7.

32. David L. Solberg, "Community-Based Spiritual Care: An Emerging Form of Pastoral Care" (D. Min. thesis., Luther Seminary, 1999).

Index

Acceptance, of terminal illness
  diagnosis, 114,115
Adler, Alfred, 2,9,30-31,61,93
Aging, crisis of, 14
AIDS (acquired immunodeficiency
  syndrome) units, in long-term care
  facilities, 145
Allers, Rudolf, 46-47
Allport, Gordon, 3,37,46
Alzheimer's disease, 68
  biomedical approach to, 69
  quality-of-life assessment in, 79
Alzheimer's disease patients, in
  long-term care facilities, 145,146
  in community-based residential
    facilities, 72-81
    activities of, 73-75
    emotions of, 75-78
    humor of, 76-78
    values of, 78-81
American Journal of Psychiatry, 3
American Psychiatric Association,
  Oskar Pfister award, 3
American Society on Aging, 143
Anger, of terminally-ill patients, 114
Anthropology, relationship with
  therapeutic goals, 12-13
Anxiety
  death-related, 54
  existential, 111-112
    of terminally-ill cancer patients,
      111-112
  ontological, 125-126,127-128
  Tillich's concept of, 111,125-126
Attitudes. *See also* Values, attitudinal
  choice of, 92-93
  toward suffering,
    49,71,104,112,145
    in dementia, 71

in terminal illness, 112-113,115
  toward unalterable fate, 127
Augustine, 30,142
Auschwitz, 3,4-5,27

Bargaining, by terminally-ill patients,
  114-115
Beck, Aaron, 122,123,132
Being, relationship with meaning,
  47-48
Bible, large-print and audio versions
  of, 154
Bible study groups, for long-term care
  facility residents, 150
Boisen, Anton, 36
Buddha, 108-109
Buhler, Charlotte, 46

Cancer, 98. *See also* Terminally-ill
  cancer patients
Caregivers, for dementia patients, 68
Centenarians, 142
Centeredness, 96,98-99
Change, 96-97
Chayefsky, Paddy, 43
Choices, 19
Clergy
  as hospice care team members,
    115-116
  involvement in community-based
    long-term care, 154-156
Cognitive-behavioral therapy, 122-123
Cognitive triad, of depression, 132
Concentration camps, Viktor Frankl's
  experiences in, 3,4-5,27,60-61,71,
    79,112,114-115,143,144
Concept of the Dead, The